Advance Acclaim for
THIRSTY FOR GOD

Unlike previous histories of spirituality, this one does not assume prior knowledge of the 2,000-year story of Christianity. It briefly yet interestingly provides the needed information about the different religious, social, theological, and institutional contexts within which diverse spiritualities have flourished. It could serve as an introduction to the history of Christianity as a whole, told from the angle which most interests contemporary students: religious affections, the reasons of the heart. The questions and suggested exercises at the end of each chapter add to the usefulness as a text. In short, this is a uniquely appealing multicultural and non-Eurocentric initiation into the study of not only Christian spirituality, but post-biblical Christianity.
    —**GEORGE LINDBECK**
      Pitkin Professor of Historical Theology
      Yale University

This is an engaging book. Brad Holt writes about spirituality with a keen contemporary sensitivity as well as a rich historical perspective. Devotional practices and spiritual exercises are introduced in their historical and theological context—useful questions and exercises follow each chapter. I can not think of a more timely topic for the American church in our post-Christian era. I have already started recommending the book to my friends.
    —**WILLIAM A. DYRNESS**
      Dean, School of Theology
      Fuller Theological Seminary

Thirsty for God is a book for seekers. For many, spirituality is a negative word, seen as a new fad or means of self-improvement. Brad Holt has done us a favor by writing this book for his course on Christian spirituality at Augsburg College. He traces the roots and growth of Christian spirituality and shows us the importance of spirituality being connected to the love of God, self, others, and the environment. Dr. Holt encourages a global dimension and states, "The study of Christian spirituality needs to be revised to include more non-Western sources, people of color, and women." *Thirsty for God* is a book long overdue.
    —**MARY R. SCHRAMM**
      Manager, St. Martin's Table

This multifaceted and global picture of Christian spirituality describes in a clear and succinct way how men and women have quenched their thirst for God. In classic fashion, it provides a seeker with carefully researched and thoroughly documented information on a subject now blossoming in popularity and widespread interest. It goes beyond merely dispensing information. Thoughtful discussion questions help the reader evaluate the spirituality approaches of various cultures and church bodies. Practical suggestions for meditation launch a seeker in the practice of Christian spirituality.

I recommend this exceptional resource for use in a congregational study group where seekers are on a serious quest for a deeper relationship with God.

—MERTON STROMMEN
Founder, Augsburg Youth and Family Institute

For those who take seriously their thirst for God and have struggled with the tension between religion and spirituality, Bradley Holt has offered a "cup of cold water." Holt offers a wealth of historical information enabling the reader to gain an insight and appreciation of Christian spirituality throughout the ages. What is especially helpful are the practical suggestions offered at the conclusion of each chapter by which one's spirituality may develop.

—DENNIS MORREIM
Author, *The Road to Recovery* and *Changed Lives*

Thirsty for God fills a gap for those who are seeking to connect their interest in contemporary spirituality with the rich and diverse spiritual traditions of Christianity. With his reflective and pastoral approach, the author accomplishes well what he sets out to do: engage the reader in conversation with Christians of the past and help each identify his or her own spiritual ancestors. Holt's sweep of history is broad and his vision wide. He is inclusive not only of the "greats" within that history, but of the "ordinary folk"; he makes an effort at identifying women wisdom figures as well as men; he concentrates not only upon Europeans, but on the peoples of Latin America, Asia, and Africa. Holt's crisp and clear prose as well as his deeply respectful ecumenical perspective makes this book a delight to read.

—EDWARD C. SELLNER
Director, Masters Program in Theology
The College of St. Catherine, St. Paul, MN.

Brad Holt has written a vital book for Lutherans who want both to tap the resources of their own tradition but also learn more about the ecumenical heritage of spirituality. In a theologically sound but nontechnical way he helps the reader access both the major writers and important techniques in a wonderfully creative way. His generous spirit gives the book a tone of exploration and openness. This is far more than "A Brief History of Christian Spirituality"; it is a reliable guide for exploring all the dimensions of Christian faith in God.

—TIMOTHY F. LULL
Academic Dean and Professor of Systematic Theology
Pacific Lutheran Theological Seminary

*A Brief
History of
Christian
Spirituality*

THIRSTY
FOR GOD

BRADLEY P. HOLT

Augsburg
MINNEAPOLIS

This book is for Linda.

THIRSTY FOR GOD
A Brief History of Christian Spirituality

Copyright © 1993 Augsburg Fortress. All rights reserved. Except for brief quotations in critical articles or reviews, no part of this book may be reproduced in any manner without prior written permission from the publisher. Write to: Permissions, Augsburg Fortress, 426 S. Fifth St., Box 1209, Minneapolis, MN 55440.

Scripture quotations are from the New Revised Standard Version Bible, copyright © 1989 by the Division of Christian Education of the National Council of the Churches of Christ in the United States of America. Used with permission.

Excerpts from the Odes of Solomon are from *The Old Testament Pseudepigrapha*, ed. James H. Charlesworth (Garden City, N.Y.: Doubleday, 1985). Used by permission of Doubleday, a division of Bantam, Doubleday, Dell Publishing Group, Inc.

Excerpts from *The Collected Works of St. John of the Cross*, tr. Kieran Kavanagh and Otilio Rodriguez, copyright © 1979 Washington Province of Discalced Carmelites, are used by permission of ICS Publications, 2131 Lincoln Rd. NE, Washington, DC 20002.

Interior design: Publishers' WorkGroup
Cover design: Catherine Reishus McLaughlin
Cover art: Rembrandt, Christ and the Woman of Samaria. Used by permission of the Metropolitan Museum of Art.

Library of Congress Cataloging-in-Publication Data

Holt, Bradley P., 1941–
   Thirsty for God : a brief history of Christian spirituality /
Bradley P. Holt.
   p.   cm.
   Includes bibliographical references and index.
   ISBN 0-8066-2640-2
   1. Spirituality—History.   I. Title.
BV4490.H67   1993
248'.09—dc20   93-17863
                                                    CIP

The paper used in this publication meets the minimum requirements of American National Standard for Information Sciences—Permanence of Paper for Printed Library Materials, ANSI Z329.48-1984.   ∞™

Manufactured in the U.S.A.   AF 9-2640
97   96   4   5   6   7   8   9   10

Contents

Preface

This book is intended for seekers. It is for people who have not yet seriously studied Christian spirituality. You may be a church member whose congregation has not taken an interest in spirituality. Or you may be a person questing for wholeness through a Twelve-Step program or the New Age movement and may wonder what Christians have to offer. Or you may simply be curious about the interest in spirituality and how it relates to Christianity.

This book was written both for the interested individual and for the classroom, whether it is in college, seminary, or church. I wrote it because there was no appropriate text for my courses in Christian Spirituality at Augsburg College. I looked in vain for a brief treatment of the Christian tradition that incorporated the features of this book: simplicity, global perspective, and practical application. I do not consider myself worthy to write this book, but someone needed to write it, so I did!

My own interest in spirituality became explicit while I was in graduate school at Yale University in the late 1960s. I had tried to find a way to write my dissertation within the field of systematic theology, but I wound up writing on the history of spirituality instead. My dear friend and mentor, Dr. Bernhard Christensen, was finishing his book *The Inward Pilgrimage* at this time. Later, teaching at the Theological College of Northern Nigeria opened my eyes to the global scope of contemporary Christianity and the strength of African Christian spiritual life.

A short introduction like this one cannot attempt to discuss all the major figures in the tradition. The choices have been very difficult but necessary for the scope of this book. Fuller treatments are noted in the bibliography, excellent guides that contain extensive detail. For the sake of simplicity, footnotes have been kept to a mimimum.

Biblical quotations are from the New Revised Standard Version unless otherwise noted. It has been my intention to use inclusive language in this account, but quotations from previous studies may not follow the standards of gender neutrality.

I want to thank a few of the many people who have helped in the years of preparing the manuscript. I thank the students in my classes for helpful

comments and suggestions; Augsburg College for a sabbatical leave spent
partly in South Africa, Namibia, and the United Kingdom; the Augsburg
Faculty Development Program, the Hoversten Peace Grant, Harriet Lystig
and Frances Holt for helping to finance that journey, Professor Andrew Walls
and the staff of the Center for the Study of Christianity in the Non-Western
World, New College, Edinburgh, and the librarians at the Augsburg library
and Luther Northwestern Seminary Library for helping me obtain materials.
Thanks to Kristin Anderson for help with the cover illustration. Special thanks
to those who read the manuscript: Cynthia Englund, Darrell Jodock, Bradley
Hanson, Eric Lund, Ryan LaHurd, Anne Julian-van Abel, Jon Fure, Carolyn
Lystig, and Lynne Lorenzen. I thank Irene Getz and Lois Torvik at Augsburg
Books. Most of all, I thank the person who has most helped to shape the
manuscript into user-friendly English, Linda Holt.

O God, you are my God, I seek you,
my soul thirsts for you;
my flesh faints for you,
as in a dry and weary land
where there is no water.

Psalm 63:1

1 | *Spirituality and Christianity*

Part of the human predicament is not always knowing what one really needs or longs for. Another part is the difficulty of acting consistently on what one does know. For example, I have had a problem listening to my body. I get tired or listless during the day and take a break to eat. Or I get upset or discouraged and eat. I smile at the refrigerator motto: "If all else fails, eat!" For a long time I did not know that my body craved water, not food. I have discovered that just plain water will usually perk me up better at mid morning or late afternoon than the various combinations of caffeine, sugar, and fat that settle on my front. I have come to recognize thirst as being different from hunger, and to respond to my body's genuine need, at least some of the time!

One of the basic premises of any spirituality is that our nonphysical selves also thirst. We may not know what we need, and we may try to satisfy our needs with possessions, foods, or relationships that do not satisfy and that may bring dangerous side effects. Christian spirituality identifies what we really long for as the living water of God, fresh and sparkling and pure. Long ago a woman from Samaria thirsted for this water.[1] She met Jesus, who saw her spiritual need and offered her living water. This water is not merely moving liquid, as she at first supposed; it is the Spirit of the living God.[2]

A second premise, crucial for Christians, is that God's love actively seeks the thirsty. It is as if wanderers in a dry land are trying to function in a state of dehydration. They do not recognize their need as thirst and may try to fulfill their need for water by eating pretzels or potato chips. God in this parable is a beautiful fountain running over with the water of life, becoming a river that offers itself to the thirsty, and longs to share its vivifying power. Here is where the metaphor of water breaks down, for water is impersonal and cannot love.

Is "Christian Spirituality" an Oxymoron?

For many people, the terms *Christian* and *spirituality* do not fit together. Many see spirituality as an alternative to Christianity, for they contrast spirituality with religion, and they see Christianity as a religion. According to

1

this view, religions have doctrines, creeds, buildings, clergy, and budgets. Such institutions are interested in their own preservation and are not much interested in helping people with their problems. Some see the Christian tradition as so entrenched in patriarchal abuse or devaluing of women that it must be abandoned. Others see Christians as unwilling to accept those who struggle with addictions to alcohol or other drugs.

Such people are eager to learn about spirituality but not about Christianity. They are on a personal search for a meaningful relationship with the sacred but are put off by the insistence on church attendance, the meager instruction in technique, and the impersonal nature of much church life. Many people have been wounded by the church, by its indifference, its gossip, its sexism, or its racism. The treasure of the gospel of Jesus is truly contained in the earthen vessels of human followers. It is the message of that gospel and the Healer to whom it points that attract people, in spite of the faults of local churches.

On the other hand, Christians, especially pastors and theologians, may be put off by the teachings found in popular books on spirituality. It may seem to them that spirituality is nothing more than the latest fad in self-improvement. "Spirituality" is a vague term people use to include anything they want. For Protestants in particular, the term is unfamiliar; it is not part of the traditional language.

Furthermore, "spirituality" looks suspicious to some Christians because it sounds like "do-it-yourself" salvation. If you only do this or that, some books suggest, you will find fulfillment or self-realization. This is very different from finding peace with God through repentance and faith in Christ.

So is it appropriate to speak of "Christian spirituality"? Yes, it is. In fact the term *spirituality* was first used among Christians. One need not be Christian to have a spirituality, but Christianity can be the basis for a vibrant and personal spirituality.

I believe that churches need to listen more to groups and individuals who are seeking a spirituality and that persons in the New Age movement and Twelve-Step groups need to give Christianity a second chance. Many churches have not responded to the longing of the human heart for an experiential knowledge of God rather than simply a "head" knowledge gained by reading books. The churches have generally done very little to help members or visitors grow in personal disciplines such as prayer and meditation or to understand the traditions concerning these central practices. Adults can be introduced to a variety of approaches, since not every person functions in the same way. At the same time, support groups are important for personal guidance. Thus churches need to encourage an individual exploration and experience of the faith in the context of the church's practice of communal worship.

Individual seekers, on the other hand, would do well to become aware of the long history of spiritual practice in the church. Like the blind person who touched one part of the elephant, one person's experience is too limited to discover reality. Previous experience through the ages serves as both an encouragement and a warning. Furthermore, churches that live up to their calling offer an individual seeker the personal community that is essential for balanced Christian spirituality.

One of the essential features of biblical spirituality is the importance of the community, the church. Another is integrating one's life in the world with one's relationship to God. A third, among many, is the personal interaction with God through all sorts of prayer. Christian spirituality includes more than an introspective search for psychological health; ideally it integrates relationships to God and creation with those to self and others.

Christian spirituality is historical and global. It is an array of twenty centuries of development. It involves global connections with others whose cultures are very different from ours in North America. I am convinced that in teaching about spirituality the churches do not sufficiently draw upon either the tradition or the sisters and brothers around the world. We need one another!

For example, Henri Nouwen, one of the best known North American writers on spirituality, remarks:

> In the free world of the United States, where most of the world's wealth is concentrated, spiritual freedom is often hard to find. Many Christians in the North are imprisoned by their fears and guilt. . . . The spiritual destiny of the people of North America is intimately connected with the spiritual destiny of the people in Latin America. I am increasingly struck by the thought that what is happening in the Christian communities of Latin America is part of God's way of calling us in the North to conversion.[3]

What Nouwen asserts here for North and South America is a specific example of what I am urging for all of us: that each of our continents has challenges—and gifts—for Christians elsewhere. We in the West do have such challenges and gifts to offer, yet it may be true that North America and Western Europe are the most in need of help. Our churches are often lethargic compared to those of Africa, Asia, and Latin America.

Our awareness is often as limited in time as it is in space. We think that the best resources must be found in the latest writer. Rather we need to look back through the centuries to learn from others of different times as well as of different continents. We need to engage in a conversation with Christians of the past, whose mistakes as well as triumphs challenge our own assumptions and life-styles.

What to Expect from This Book

I am inviting you, the reader, to an intercontinental and intergenerational conversation about spirituality.

This book is an attempt to survey the varieties of Christian spirituality in both space and time. From a late twentieth-century American perspective, it looks back in time and around the continents to point out what is valuable for thirsty persons of our time. It tells the multicultural story of Christian history as it relates to spirituality.

After a preliminary discussion of the term *spirituality* and an overview of the Christian community on a global scale (in this chapter), our discussion will focus on the Bible, the essential literary source of Christian spirituality (chapter 2). In succeeding chapters we will explore the early centuries, the medieval age, the Reformation, the "modern" period, and the twentieth century. The last chapter will draw together themes and suggestions for the future.

Discussion questions are located at the end of each chapter. Spiritual exercises relating to the subject of the chapter are also suggested. Try them out! Keep an open-minded attitude. Each person has different needs in terms of practice. These suggestions may widen your span or deepen your experience. You may discover riches you had not expected.

The movements and individuals selected for this book reflect my vision of spirituality. More will be said about this later, but for now, let me indicate some criteria for choosing the subject matter that follows. I have included the most influential figures whom any history of Christian spirituality must include, for example, Augustine, Teresa of Avila, and John of the Cross. But I have also gone outside the usual "canon" to include Protestants and Orthodox as well as Catholics, more women than is customary, and non-Western Christians.

The tradition includes some well-known names, such as Augustine, Francis, and Teresa, for example. But it also includes the ways of countless ordinary people whose names have been forgotten. What is commonly called "popular piety" is also part of this story. The spirituality that gets written in a "spiritual classic" both reflects and influences common Christians. Some of this book will describe popular movements such as charismatic Christianity, Pietism, or Twelve-Step spirituality. A great deal of it will recount the stories and writings of the "elite" who have influenced many others by the potency of their devotion.

Sometimes I will include matters of general history or church history for background, even though these are not strictly matters of "spirituality." It is important to be reminded about the context that shaped the story of Christian spirituality. I have prepared a time line as an appendix, p. 131, so that the sequence of writers is clear. Consult the glossary of specialized terms when a word confuses you and the index for finding the pages where the authors or subjects are discussed.

Christian "Spirituality" Means Walking
in the Spirit

Spirituality—this ambiguous, six-syllable term is new to many and objectionable to some. Although it is a clumsy word, it is used so much because it seems to do a task that no other word does. *Religion* for many people connotes an established system and institution, whereas *spirituality* implies personal involvement. "Spirituality" is a transreligious word; it is not tied to one single faith. Thus one can speak of Hindu or Muslim spirituality, or even spirituality not rooted in a particular religion. In earlier centuries, many Christians used the words *devotion* or *piety*. Unfortunately these older terms have developed a flavor of otherworldly sentimentality. *Spirituality* need not have this connotation and is more clearly inclusive of daily life in the world.

Spirituality is easily misunderstood. It is commonly used, for example, to refer not to a type or style, but to a degree of "spiritualness," so that it can be measured like temperature or humidity. This usage has the negative result that people tend to measure themselves or others as being more spiritual or less spiritual, and can even use the term as a club to batter others thought to be less spiritual than they are themselves. I will avoid this use of the term.

From a Christian perspective, *spirituality* calls us to recognize the importance of its root term, *spirit,* an important biblical word. In both Hebrew and Greek, the same word (*ruach* and *pneuma,* respectively) is used for breath, wind, and spirit. The Bible refers both to human spirit and to divine Spirit. How one understands spirit will determine how one understands spirituality. For example, if *spirit* is separated from physical reality, in a realm of its own, apart from the daily life of human experience, the resulting spirituality will become an escape into another world. But if God created the world good, and later became flesh, as the Gospel of John asserts, then spirit is a dimension of reality compatible with physical existence. Humans are not divided but, rather, are unities of body, mind, and spirit. The result is that spirituality has a much more wholistic and down-to-earth meaning. It encompasses the whole of human life and will develop in a variety of styles, depending on cultures, denominations, personalities, and gifts.

If we look back in history, Roman Catholic theology first used the term *spirituality* in the way we understand it today. For most of the centuries of the church, theologians included the practice of Christianity in their discussions of doctrine. But in the eighteenth and nineteenth centuries "mystical theology" and "ascetical theology" became specialized fields. The first described the teachings of the mystics, the extraordinary Christians of the tradition; the second discussed the path of ordinary Christian disciplines. In the twentieth century, these two subdisciplines combined into one: "spiritual theology" or "spirituality." Various schools of spirituality were recognized, which corresponded to the better-known religious orders. Thus Catholics began to write about Jesuit (or Ignatian) spirituality, Franciscan spirituality, Carmelite spirituality, and so on. Eventually a spirituality for the laity was also discussed.

In the first half of the twentieth century, Roman Catholic theologians assumed a number of ideas: that only Roman Catholics were genuine Christians, that spirituality grows out of the doctrines of theology, rather than vice versa, that the members of religious orders have a better track to perfection than the laity, and that the goal of all spirituality is the mystical vision of God. Because the Second Vatican Council (1962-65) produced a refreshing reassessment of Catholic faith, some of these assumptions are being questioned.

Only in the past thirty years or so have Protestants used the term *spirituality*, and the reasons are partly due to basic disagreements with some of the Catholic assumptions. But the ecumenical advance in the years since Vatican II has increased the conversation between the two traditions. Now there are studies describing the distinctive types of spirituality in the Protestant denominations just as there are in the Catholic orders. Here are two recent descriptions of spirituality from *Westminster Dictionary of Christian Spirituality:*

> Prayer in Christian theology and experience is more than pleading or petition; it is our whole relation to God. And spirituality concerns the way in which prayer influences conduct, our behaviour and manner of life, our attitudes to other people. It is often best studied in biographies, but clearly it shapes dogmas, inspires movements and builds institutions.[4]

> SPIRITUALITY. This is a word which has come much into vogue to describe those attitudes, beliefs, practices which animate people's lives and help them to reach out towards super-sensible realities. . . . This means that Christian spirituality is not simply for "the interior life" or the inward person, but as much for the body as for the soul, and is directed to the implementation of both the commandments of Christ, to love God and our neighbor. Indeed, our love, like God's, should extend to the whole of creation. Christian spirituality at its most authentic includes in its scope both humanity and nature.[5]

My own understanding of the term in the Christian context is that it refers in the first place to lived experience. "If we live by the Spirit, let us also be guided by the Spirit," Paul writes (Gal. 5:25). The starting point is the spirit of Christ living in the person, but the person is always considered in the context of a community, the body of Christ. Spirituality describes a particular *style* of Christian discipleship. For example, Jesuits and Lutherans and feminists each have a particular combination of themes and practices that make them distinctive. Note that each member of these groups has individual gifts and traits as well. Each group or person has a distinct flavor. This book will give you a small taste of many flavors.

Second, I understand spirituality to refer to a theological field, an academic discipline, which might better be called "spiritual theology" as opposed to "doctrinal" or "systematic" theology. This field attempts to describe and classify, to understand and evaluate, various types of Christian spirituality. It also creatively proposes ways for the Christian tradition to grow in the writer's own time and place. *Thirsty for God* is an introductory example of such an enterprise.

The Value of Studying the Global Christian Tradition

A living tradition is a self-critical developing stream, not a moribund repetition of the past. Tradition is the shoulder of previous experience on which we stand as we reach upward for what is new. Education involves studying the various traditions that have shaped a community, pondering the problems of continuity and change, and making decisions about adopting or rejecting elements of those traditions. Tradition is thus much wider than "customs"; it includes narratives, doctrines, and values. "Tradition is the living faith of the dead, traditionalism is the dead faith of the living."[6]

Citizens of the United States, for example, are in the process of reevaluating the impact of Christopher Columbus, the beliefs of the drafters of the nation's founding documents, and the results of the Vietnam War. Some elements of American tradition are very precious and deserve honor, but others, such as racism and greed, show that the nation needs repentance just as individuals do, and that new attitudes and practices are in order.

The Christian community lives as an inheritor of almost two millennia of thought, action, and prayer by people seeking to live in the power of the Holy Spirit. Great saints have exemplified the courage and love of Jesus, being living witnesses of God's power to redeem. But the history of Christianity is also marked by continual departures from the way of its Lord, of social and personal injustice, error, and violence. Therefore being heirs of a tradition does not mean that we approve of everything in it. Rather, it means that we sift out what is valuable from what is not and creatively develop neglected strands of thought.

It is vitally important for Christian spirituality today that we take a wide view of that tradition and of the global family of Christians, not simply enshrining the small strand of tradition that may be familiar from our home, congregation, or ethnic group. The sweep of that tradition will open our eyes to wide resources of spirituality and give guidance for our own choices.

Perhaps no one has so pointedly stated the need for reading books from previous ages as C. S. Lewis in his introduction to a fourth-century theological/ spiritual work of the young Athanasius.

> Every Age has its own outlook. It is specially good at seeing certain truths and specially liable to make certain mistakes. We all, therefore, need the books that will correct the characteristic mistakes of our own period. And that means the

old books. . . . Nothing strikes me more when I read the controversies of past
ages than the fact that both sides were usually assuming without question a
good deal which we should now absolutely deny. . . . We may be sure that the
characteristic blindness of the twentieth century—the blindness about which
posterity will ask, "But how *could* they have thought that?"—lies where we
never suspected it. . . . None of us can fully escape this blindness, but we shall
certainly increase it, and weaken our guard against it, if we read only modern
books. . . . The only palliative is to keep the clean sea breeze of the centuries
blowing through our minds, and this can be done only by reading old books.
Not, of course, that there is any magic about the past. People were no cleverer
then than they are now; they made as many mistakes as we. But not the *same*
mistakes. They will not flatter us in the errors we are already committing; and
their own error, being now open and palpable, will not endanger us. Two heads
are better than one, not because either is infallible, but because they are unlikely
to go wrong in the same direction.[7]

For perspective on the assumptions of the spirituality of our own age,
assumptions that need to be questioned, nothing is better than reading the
spiritual classics from the past and spiritual writings from other continents.

The first function of a study of the tradition and the present-day Christian
family is to make us aware of our own narrowness, our own parochialism.
Knowing a larger part of the whole tradition gives us better questions to ask
of the fads of the present. We are endangered not only with ethnocentrism,
judging all things by the customs of our own ethnic group, but also "chron-
ocentrism," judging all previous ages as inferior to our own.

The second function of the study of the tradition is to display the variety
of approaches to Christian spirituality. Too often we have thought that there
is only one form of Christian prayer or one way of following Jesus. The
tradition shows over time a great cloud of witnesses, a treasure house of
approaches to living in discipleship to Jesus.

Varieties of approach include differences of emphasis on different biblical
truths, such as we have in different denominations. Just as there are four
Gospels, each bringing out different perspectives on the same Redeemer, so
our denominations crystallize around different starting points within the story
of the one Christ.

The varieties also include national cultural differences. Christianity began
in a Jewish setting, very soon became Greco-Roman, Syrian, Armenian, and
Ethiopian, and today is found in virtually every major cultural group in the
world.

And of course the differences are personal. The Christian God is a respecter
of the variety of personality, so that women and men of every type have
followed the Way and left markers for introverts and extroverts, for people
who mostly use their emotions and for others who use their intellect to face
the world. These can be seen, for example, in women as diverse as Teresa

of Avila and Teresa of Calcutta, and in men with different temperaments, such as Francis of Assisi and Thomas Aquinas.

What is the effect of studying this great variety of Christian spirituality, past and present? It is to widen the options available, to loosen our grip on nonessentials, to increase our wonder at the fellowship of which we are a part.

In its third function, the Christian tradition not only displays variety, but also presents norms or boundaries for that variety. Although there are many ways of living a spiritual life in the power of the gospel, there is only one God, one Lord, one baptism. The norms of genuine Christian spirituality are preeminently the Scriptures but also the creeds of the early church. As individuals we are free to question these norms, yet they give identity and continuity to the community over time and space.

Theological norms are the statements of worldview, statements about the way things are, that form the skeleton on which the flesh of spirituality depends. For example, some people in early centuries thought that spirit was better than matter and began to forbid eating, having sex, and bathing. It was the faith that God created the world good that helped to hold this dualistic spirituality in check.

Yet there are practical norms for spirituality in addition to the theological ones. These determine how helpful a particular proposal will be in a given situation. A manner of shaping the Christian life may be perfectly orthodox doctrinally but may not meet the needs of people. This was common experience in colonial days in Africa, when European models were only partially helpful for new African Christians. Today Africans are seeking truly indigenous styles of spirituality that do not require them to become culturally European in order to become religiously Christian.

Christians have a very big playing field, but there are also boundaries outside which the game is no longer Christian. In our day these lines are not always as clear as they seemed in past centuries, and many think that this is appropriate and gives space for exploration. Nevertheless, not every spirituality is a Christian spirituality, and that distinction is necessary for the identity and integrity of the tradition. My view is that Christians need to have their ears and hearts open to learn from other religious and cultural traditions, for example the Native American traditions, but not lose the centrality of Jesus Christ and the Bible as normative for their spirituality.

Christian History Looks Like
an Hourglass

Christianity is not a European religion, although today many people view it as such. The story of its expansion shows that Christianity is as truly Asian or African as European. Jesus and his disciples were not Europeans, in spite of countless paintings that suggest that they were. Their culture was Middle

Eastern Judaism, and their biological inheritance was from the ancient He-
brews, whose roots have no contact with Europe.

Perhaps we think of Jesus as European because most American Jews today
have come from Europe, and we assume wrongly that he must have looked
like them. In fact, Jews come in all colors, and it is not clear what color
Jesus' skin might have been.

We may simplify Christian expansion into four main stages. First came a
time of expansion to three continents: Asia, Africa, and Europe.

We read in Acts that the gospel spread from Jerusalem to Judea, to Samaria,
and to the ends of the world. The narrative introduces an African into the
account (chap. 8) even before Paul travels to Europe with the good news
(chap. 16).

With good roads and busy trading routes, Christianity spread very rapidly
in all directions. In the first century it probably reached Roman Britain as
well as Egypt, Arabia, and Armenia. Armenia was the first of the nations to
declare itself Christian. The Mar Thoma Church in India and the Ethiopian
Church also claim to date back to the first century, and we can be sure that
they have their roots in this ancient period, even if the date accepted by
Western historians is somewhat later.

So, if Christianity stretched from India and even China in the east to Britain
in the west, from the Danube in the north to Ethiopia in the south, it is clear
that at first Christianity was not just a Roman faith, nor even a European one,
but truly a faith found in many cultures on three continents.

But a withdrawal marked the second period. After the establishment of
Christianity by Rome and Constantinople in the fourth century, the doctrinal
splits of the fifth century, and the rise of Islam in the seventh century, the
African and Asian churches were reduced to small minorities or completely
disbanded.

The emperors after Constantine gradually moved from recognizing Christianity as a legal religion to making it the official state religion of the empire.
This Byzantine connection between emperor and Christianity led to two un-
intended results. First, the rulers of other empires—Persia, for example—
began to see the faith as the state religion of their enemies and thus began to
persecute its followers as disloyal to their homelands. Second, it meant that
a complaint against the church became a complaint against the state, and vice
versa. Doctrinal disputes became political matters. Some of the peoples who
were ruled from Constantinople became ripe for conversion to Islam because
of their unhappiness with the rule of the distant emperors.

The Council of Chalcedon in A.D. 451 defined the teaching about the
person of Christ, his divine and human natures, in a way that many Africans
and Asians refused to accept. They were branded Monophysites or Nestorians,
even though it is questionable that they differed fundamentally from the
powerful churches related to Constantinople and Rome, who accepted the

Chalcedonian definition. The definition stated that Jesus Christ is one person with two "natures," human and divine. The Monophysites rejected the idea of two "natures" and insisted that Jesus Christ had one nature.

Many Christians who were alienated from the emperor in Constantinople by these doctrinal disputes welcomed the arrival of the Arabs in the seventh century and eventually adopted Islam. They did so, not at the point of the sword, but over time, under social, political, and economic pressure from the Muslim governments.

During this second period, Christianity was gradually indigenized in Europe, where it continued to expand. For more than a thousand years this faith dominated southern Europe; the northern peoples of Russia and Scandinavia were won over only after kings' decisions around A.D. 1000. Christian theology and spirituality came to be shaped by Europe's various cultures—Greek, Roman, Celtic, Germanic, Slavic, and Norse. For example, the celebration of Christmas on December 25 and the use of a Christmas tree or Yule log are adaptations of Christianity to previous European religions.

It came to be assumed that Christianity and European culture were one and the same; the universal character of Christianity was in danger of being lost. Some theologians even argued that since other peoples had not believed the gospel at Pentecost in the first century, it was useless to give them a second chance now, for God had obviously chosen the Europeans as his own and left the others out in the cold!

A new expansion from Europe to all six continents characterized the third period, from the sixteenth to the mid twentieth century. First Roman Catholic and later Protestant missionaries took the message of the cross to all six continents. Further, the vast emigration of Europeans to the Americas, Australia, and South Africa made Christianity dominant in those areas. The political background of this expansion included European imperialism, first Portuguese and Spanish, then Dutch, English, and French, and finally the economic and cultural dominance of the United States.

Christianity spread by emigration and by mission work from the North Atlantic, in a Europeanized form, often with little regard for the cultures and religions it replaced. This period was fundamental to our present situation in providing both its possibility and its problems: the possibility of a world Christian community, not just a "white man's religion," and the problems of a distorted gospel that has suffered from European hegemony, racism, tribalism, and sexism.

Today, in the fourth period of development, the spread of Christianity is not only from the Europeans. The churches of most countries are involved in evangelization domestically or internationally. The churches of Africa and Asia are also seeking ways to evaluate European forms of the gospel and shuck off those aspects of Christianity that are tainted by a colonial past. The churches of Latin America are struggling to overcome the economic imbalances rooted in the colonial period. Christianity is weakening in its old strongholds and growing in the continents of Africa, Latin America, and Asia. This century, which was predicted to be the one in which all religions would die out, has proved on the contrary to be a time of rejuvenation for all of the major world religions, including Christianity, in the non-Western world.

One may view the story of Christianity as a sort of hourglass, with wide geographical extent in the early and most recent centuries, but a narrow stem of European isolation in the middle. It is obvious then that a sound approach to the story of Christian spirituality must take into account movements and individuals outside of Europe. My aim here is to bring together two fields of knowledge that do not often connect: first, historians of Christian spirituality, who often concentrate on Europeans; and second, scholars of missions and new indigenous movements. The early non-Western spiritualities are as important to the study as the recent ones, and I will discuss them in chapter 3.

As we look back on this story we see that Christianity has been crossing cultural boundaries from its start on the Day of Pentecost up to the present. The translations of the Bible are a witness to this, with today's consciousness of "contextualization" its climax. "Contextualization" is the process in which Christianity speaks to a group of people in language and symbols with which they are at home, and they in turn express their Christian faith within their culture. The model for this process is seen to be the Word of God, who became fully human in Jesus of Nazareth, who was incarnated in human flesh and in a particular history and culture.

This account is designed mainly for North American readers, but the basic idea applies everywhere. Christians in Europe, Latin America, Africa, Asia, and Australia and the South Pacific—all of us—will gain from sharing with one another and from studying the spirituality of the present along with that of the past, which informs our present.

The Author's Perspective

None of us is neutral about matters he or she deems important. Academic teaching that aims at objectivity still is shot through with the values of researchers, writers, and professors. The fact that we each see things from our own perspective does not imply that the world of learning is hopelessly chaotic and subjective, but rather that we need to take into account the personal values and commitments of the writer or speaker and then seek to learn, even if our own perspective is quite different. We must take what is good and leave the rest.

As a way of introducing myself, I might list some important factors that have shaped my views of the world. I am a Protestant, a Lutheran who sees great value in the Orthodox and Catholic traditions, and who sees Jesus Christ, the gospel, and the Bible as normative for interpreting the Christian spiritual traditions. My spouse Linda and our three children, Olaf, Karin, and Paul have helped me to grow up, to accept myself, and to take responsibility.

I am a North American male of Scandinavian heritage who has been changed by nearly a decade of life in Africa, teaching at the Theological College of Northern Nigeria. I believe that the study of Christian spirituality needs to be revised to include more non-Western sources, people of color, and women.

Having studied for many years in institutions of higher education, my approach to religion has been very intellectual, academic "left brain." My interest in spirituality is due in part to the needs of the other side of my human nature, the experiential, emotional, spontaneous "right brain." On one level, this book is an attempt to bring these two together.

• DISCUSSION QUESTIONS

1. Do you see North Americans as spiritually needy or thirsty?
2. How would you define spirituality?
3. How does Christianity relate to spirituality?
4. What evidence can be offered that Christianity is not European? What difference does it make?

• EXERCISES: Silence and Meditation

1. One may think of silence as giving "loving attention" to God and to oneself. Determine to spend some time each day in quietness. Choose a place, either inside, for example, in a favorite chair, or outside, where you can walk, jog, or bike. Deliberately become aware of your body's rhythms, of breathing, heartbeat, and muscle tension. Do not try to control your thoughts, but remain in a state of relaxed alertness in the presence of God. If you find your thoughts turning to upcoming activities, sexual fantasies, worries, or any other "static," take the distraction as a sign of something coming to the surface, but return to your silence without being perturbed or blaming yourself.

As you repeat this exercise, you will be able to calm and center yourself more quickly and appreciate the silence for longer periods of time. This focusing in silence is a fundamental discipline of spiritualities and provides the basis for others that require focusing or paying attention.

2. Meditation is focusing one's thoughts while at the same time being open to inspirations as they come. The object of meditation may be a natural phenomenon. For example, one can sit by a lake, a seacoast, a meadow, or a forest and quietly observe and ponder. Or one can meditate on an event in one's own life or that of a biblical figure or saint. For Christians, meditating on Jesus and the events of his life is central. The meditative reading of the Bible will be described as the exercise in our next chapter.

• AIDS FOR THE EXERCISES

Foster, Richard J. *Celebration of Discipline: The Path to Spritual Growth*, 2d ed. San
   Francisco: Harper, 1988.
————. *Challenge of the Disciplines*. San Francisco: Harper, 1989.
   These books contain sound advice about most of the exercises in these chapters.
   I highly recommend them.
Hanson, Bradley. *The Call of Silence: Discovering Christian Meditation*. Minneapolis:
   Augsburg, 1980.
Hulme, William E. *Celebrating God's Presence: A Guide to Christian Meditation*.
   Minneapolis: Augsburg, 1988.
Klug, Ron, and Lyn Klug. *Faithful Hearts, Faithful Hands*. Rejoice Curriculum for
   Adults. Minneapolis: Augsburg, 1992.

• SUGGESTED READING

Original Texts

The most comprehensive set of primary sources is found in the Paulist
Press series *Classics of Western Spirituality*. The translations are recent, with
introductory essays to set the context for these writings. The set will include
more than fifty volumes when it is complete.

Comprehensive Surveys

Jones, Cheslyn, Geoffrey Wainwright, and Edward Yarnold, eds. *The Study of
   Spirituality*. New York: Oxford University Press, 1986.
   This is the single most helpful volume for reading further in the history of
   Christian spirituality. The thick paperback also includes sections on the theology
   of spirituality and on pastoral spirituality. It contains extensive bibliographies on
   all of the figures discussed. It is a comprehensive reference written by many
   authors.
McGinn, Bernard, and John Meyendorff, eds., *Christian Spirituality: Origins to the
   Twelfth Century;* Jill Raitt, ed., *Christian Spirituality: High Middle Ages and
   Reformation;* Louis Dupre and Don E. Saliers, eds., *Christian Spirituality: Post
   Reformation and Modern* (vols. 16-18 of World Spirituality). New York:
   Crossroad, 1985-89.
   This three-volume collection of articles gives a comprehensive survey of the
   tradition.

Shorter Surveys

Maas, Robin, and Gabriel O'Donnell, O.P., eds. *Spiritual Traditions for the
   Contemporary Church*. Nashville: Abingdon, 1990.
Tugwell, Simon, O.P. *Ways of Imperfection*. Springfield, Ill.: Templegate, 1985.
Williams, Rowan. *Christian Spirituality: A Theological History from the New
   Testament to Luther and St. John of the Cross*. Atlanta: John Knox, 1980.
   These one-volume surveys are very useful. The first includes exercises for the

reader, while the last two have particular emphases on the cross and on living with imperfection.

A Dictionary
Wakefield, Gordon S., ed. *Westminster Dictionary of Christian Spirituality.* Philadelphia: Westminster, 1983.
Short entries on most topics are included in this very helpful reference.

About the "Hourglass"
Hood, Robert E. *Must God Remain Greek? Afro Cultures and God Talk.* Minneapolis: Fortress, 1990. A challenge to Eurocentric views of Christianity.
Latourette, Kenneth Scott. *A History of the Expansion of Christianity.* 7 vols. Grand Rapids: Zondervan, 1970 (reprint of 1937-45 ed.).
This old classic describes in detail all of the ages up to World War II.

About the Christian Tradition
Gonzolez, Justo L. *A History of Christian Thought.* 3 vols. New York: Abingdon, 1970-75.
This is a very good survey of the tradition for beginners.
Pelikan, Jaroslav. *The Christian Tradition.* 5 vols. Chicago: University of Chicago, 1971-89.
For advanced students of the tradition.

About the Academic Study of Spirituality
Hanson, Bradley C., ed. *Modern Christian Spirituality: Methodological and Historical Essays.* American Academy of Religion Studies in Religion, no. 62. Atlanta: Scholars Press, 1990.
Those interested in the academic side of spirituality will find the main issues debated here.

2 | Four Relationships in the Bible

The foundational documents of Christian spirituality are the Holy Scriptures. All later developments have their matrix in the divine-human dialogue recorded in the Bible. Though it has been interpreted in widely divergent ways, the canon of Scripture is recognized as the norm by all major Christian traditions. But to set forth the teaching of the Bible on Christian spirituality would fill many books. The richness of its text is endless.

In this chapter I have selected some of the biblical teachings on the four basic relationships that constitute spirituality: our relationships to God, to self, to others, and to creation. The selection of concepts and passages reflects my understanding of what is most important for these themes and what I see as having been neglected in congregational teaching.

The discussion assumes a preliminary acquaintance with the Bible. If you are not familiar with the Scriptures, reading a brief introduction to the Bible will be helpful. See the end of this chapter for suggested reading.

The Bible is not simply one book but a whole library, written and collected over centuries by many writers in different situations. Thus it must be interpreted with care, not taking one verse as the "answer" to a present-day problem, but looking for the main themes of the whole.

The Bible functions in a number of ways in its approach to spirituality. First, it is food for spirituality. Much of the Bible is narrative, and the stories illumine the daily walk. Meditative reading of the Bible; listening to it preached; or seeing it portrayed in a film, play, or painting can feed the soul. The Bible portrays God, Jesus, and the Holy Spirit in ways that convey good news to the reader or listener. The Bible becomes a living word from God when the Spirit speaks directly to our needs.

The Psalms have a special place in Christian spirituality as model prayers from all emotional levels. Their general character makes them appropriate for individuals with specific, contemporary problems. The Psalms have been sung in distinctive ways by Catholic monks, by Anglicans, and by Presbyterians, and are used by members of all denominations in public worship and private devotion.

The Bible is also a norm or standard for the theology and ethics that interact so profoundly with spirituality. That is, the basic worldview and values of

16

Christianity are taught and demonstrated in the Bible. They function as presuppositions for all Christian writing. For example, the Bible teaches that God created the world and declared it good. It teaches that God became human in Jesus and that his death and resurrection form the basis for human salvation. It teaches that God's love operates in our lives through the Holy Spirit, poured out at Pentecost.

The Bible Calls Us to Welcome God's Love and to Love God

When Jesus is asked to name the greatest commandment, he quotes from Deuteronomy (see Mark 12:28-31; Deut. 6:4-5). The first is to love the LORD your God with all your heart, soul, mind, and strength. Whatever else the Bible says about God that is relevant for spirituality, this is fundamental. God is to be loved with the whole self.

But who is this God? It is the God whose blazing love first created and then redeemed us. This God tenderly, jealously, sometimes wrathfully, sometimes joyously loved ancient Israel. This God took human flesh, was mocked and was killed to set free all peoples from sin, evil, and death. The simplest description of this One is "God is love." Spirituality is welcoming this love into our lives; allowing it to change our habits, feelings, and thoughts; and thus returning the love to God who started it.

Fundamental to any particular spirituality is its view of God, intellectually and emotionally. The intellectual side comes out in doctrines about God's nature. The emotional side comes out in prayers of celebration and mourning. Both sides are expressed in stories and metaphors, which abound in the Bible.

The Hebrew Bible or Old Testament gives us the basic understanding of God that dominates the whole tradition. The delicate balance of what can be known of God and what is beyond human understanding is expressed in a number of ways. God speaks to Moses, for example, "face to face, as one speaks to a friend," but when Moses wants to see God's glory, he is told, "you cannot see my face; for no one shall see me and live" (Ex. 33:11, 20).

Isaiah likewise expresses a very definite claim to know the character of God, while reserving God's mystery:

Have you not known? Have you not heard?
The LORD is the everlasting God,
  the Creator of the ends of the earth.
He does not faint and grow weary;
  his understanding is unsearchable.
He gives power to the faint,
  and strengthens the powerless. (Isa. 40:28-29)

The relationship to God in prayer that is portrayed in the Bible also shares this tension between the known and the unknown. The Bible both teaches about prayer and illustrates it. God is One who can be addressed by humans and who addresses them. Prayers have great variety in the Bible, showing that there is no one form of address acceptable to the Almighty. Moses and Abraham see God as a friend and sometimes argue or barter with him. Job boldly accuses God. The Psalms contain bitter laments and joyful praises. Jesus prays for healings, gives thanks, submits to the Father's will, and calls out in forsakenness on the cross. Paul is lifted to the third heaven and cannot tell what he saw. In all of these we see God as the known and the unknown. This tension will later show itself in the history of spirituality as the *Kataphatic* and *apophatic* approaches to God (see pp. 48-49).

God in the Old Testament is known as the one who led the people out of slavery, who entered into covenants with individuals and the people of Israel, who revealed the Ten Commandments, who spoke through the prophets, and yet said,

> For as the heavens are higher than the earth,
> so are my ways higher than your ways,
> and my thoughts than your thoughts. (Isa. 55:9)

Insofar as God is known, God is seen as creator of the world (Gen. 1–2 et al.), liberator of Israel (Ex. 1–15), judge of all people (Ps. 96), savior of the faithful (Ps. 27), and Holy One (Isa. 6). These universal metaphors are supplemented by a number of more personal ones. God is Friend, Father, Mother, Husband. Further, God is compared to nonhuman parts of creation: God is mother bear, mother eagle, a lion, a rock, a fortress, and fire. The images of God all fall short yet are essential for human understanding. God is none of the things listed; God is not male or female. Yet God's personal, holy, living character is important for both Jews and Christians.

The New Testament builds on the Old Testament picture, but with a breath-taking assertion: God became incarnate in a human being! It is not that the Old Testament God is a God of wrath, while the New Testament shows a God of mercy, for both aspects of God can be seen in both Testaments. But the New Testament claims that the love of God for humanity was so great that God condescended to take human form in Jesus of Nazareth. This action affirms the goodness of creation as stated in Genesis 1 and affirms the value of human beings and human culture. For marred by evil as people may be, God entered the human story in a particular place and time.

Jesus himself describes God as a shepherd seeking one lost sheep, as a woman seeking a lost coin, as a father welcoming home a lost son. He addresses God as *Abba*, the Aramaic word for a father addressed by a small child. The closest we may have is "Dad" or "Daddy." Thus Jesus lived out an intimate relation to God, modeling prayer and obedience to his own followers, but also inviting them to share in the oneness he experienced with the Father.

Paul the apostle writes that God declares sinners righteous and through the Holy Spirit also indwells them, giving spiritual gifts and producing spiritual fruit. He brings us back to the issue of God's revelation and God's mystery. He is very confident of some truths, for example, when he writes, "For I am convinced that neither death, nor life, nor angels, nor rulers, nor things present, nor things to come, nor powers, nor height, nor depth, nor anything else in all creation, will be able to separate us from the love of God in Christ Jesus our Lord" (Rom. 8:38-39). But just a short while later, after writing about the will of God for Jews and Gentiles, he concludes, "O the depth of the riches and wisdom and knowledge of God! How unsearchable are his judgments and how inscrutable his ways! . . . For from him and through him and to him are all things. To him be the glory forever. Amen" (Rom. 11:33, 36).

The Bible Calls Us to Love Ourselves

The second great commandment according to Jesus is to "Love your neighbor as yourself" (Mark 12:31; see Lev. 19:18). The main point is love of neighbor, but implied is love of self. Some recent writers have gone overboard in trying to correct a misleading teaching about the self by making this commandment say, "Look out for number one." You cannot love your neighbor, they say, unless you love yourself first. So forget about your neighbor's needs until your own psychological problems are worked out. Give yourself all that your heart desires, and do not concern yourself with the poor.

Such teaching goes directly against what it is meant to interpret. Yet Jesus did not say, "love your neighbor and hate yourself." A proper concern for the self is the standard of care for the neighbor here. A distinction must be made between love for oneself and selfishness. The former involves care, nurture, responsibility, and faithfulness; the latter is exploitative and idolatrous. To love oneself rightly is neither to grab from others to satisfy one's desires, nor to neglect the care we all need physically, psychologically, and spiritually.

The Bible does not define the self, but describes the relations people have with God, others, and creation. Psalm 139 is a meditation on the wonders of God's relation to the self, in God's creative knowledge and ubiquity. Genesis describes the person in terms of a body with the breath of life from God. This breath is the same word as "spirit." The Bible generally views a person as a unity of body, soul, mind, heart, and spirit. It does not separate these elements the way some philosophers have tended to do. Thus the self in the Bible is the whole person—intellect, will, emotions, conscious and unconscious, social and private, whatever distinctions have been made. It is this whole self that is called upon to love, serve, and praise God.

The human being is seen in the Bible as someone made in the image and likeness of God. It is this creature of great dignity and value who is also a fallen person, subject to sin and evil. The Bible describes human bondage and promises freedom. Thus the integration and healing of the self is implicit in the message of the Bible, in such explicit teachings as redemption, liberation, forgiveness, and resurrection.

Throughout the Bible people are called to repent from evil. In the New Testament the most common word for repentance means turning around, changing direction. By God's grace, human beings not only perceive some of what alienates them from God, but also receive new life, new direction, new birth.

The Bible Calls Us to Love Others

When Jesus explained the second great commandment, he told the story of a Samaritan who helped a bleeding man on the road. The vision of Christian spirituality is not only "my God and I," but the world of need in which Christians have always lived. Not only caring for the poor, but standing up for those who are being treated unjustly, is part of the Christian life.

Different kinds of love are called for in different situations. Love for Somalians whom we have never seen except on television calls for practical aid but no personal relationship. Among those we know, our community of faith, our family, and our friends are special types of relationships that call for more intimate kinds of love.

Christian spirituality has a special place for other people who share the faith. It is not only personal but communal. The Bible does not know of separating individuals from the people of Israel or from the church; our relations with God are as members of a body, not as isolated individuals. It is as a people that we celebrate the Lord's Supper and share in Christ's body and blood. It is the community that is Christ's body, not an individual. The gifts of the Spirit are given to the community, not just to individuals.

Families are important groups for spiritual nurture. The compassion and trust we show one another shape the lives of children for years to come. It is in the family that most of us learn to pray, to read the Bible devotionally, to forgive one another, to assume our responsibilities.

Spiritual friends are also important in Christian growth. Aside from the community in general, individual guides and companions can help us see ourselves in ways that we cannot see on our own. It is when someone else has heard about our sins that their assurance of God's forgiveness has power for us. The word of grace is heard more credibly from another than a self-absolution.

The field of Christian ethics studies our relation to other persons most directly. The complex ethical problems facing Christians today force us to listen carefully to the specialists who remind us of the context and the specifics of the Christian tradition that undergird us in making concrete decisions. It is important not to separate ethics from spirituality, lest spirituality be a private escape from the real world, a self-fulfillment at the cost of others. Ethics and spirituality belong together.

The Bible Calls Us to Care
for the Earth

The two creation accounts in Genesis (1:1–2:4a; 2:4b-25) affirm the goodness of the world and human existence. The first account of seven days repeatedly proclaims "God saw that it was good," and the second also makes clear God's approval. Both urge care for the natural world. Modern society has distorted and disregarded our accountability, as we exploit the earth for only human interest. The basis for Christian understanding of the world is the assertion that creation is good but is not God. The beauty and power of nature have led some to worship it; however, the Bible reminds us to worship the Creator, not the creature. The transience and cruelty of nature have caused some to despise and mistreat it, but the Bible reminds us to treat it as good caretakers or stewards.

Christian spirituality has not always given proper attention to the natural world. The influence of Neo-Platonism and other philosophies has been to view the world as an uncomfortable and transient prison. The ambiguity of the word *world* in the Bible has permitted this distortion. Especially in John, the term *world* can be used for humanity organized against God, or as 1 John has it, "all that is in the world—the desire of the flesh, the desire of the eyes, the pride in riches—comes not from the Father but from the world" (2:16). Obviously the writer is not talking about the same world God loves in John 3:16. "For God so loved the world that he gave his only Son, so that everyone who believes in him may not perish but may have eternal life."

So the term *world* has at least three meanings. It can refer to the created world that God called good in Genesis 1, or it can refer to humanity, as in John 3:16. Finally, it can refer to human evil, and it is this usage that has sometimes led to distortions in Christian spirituality. Both Catholic monks and Protestant Pietists have sought to love God and not love the world. But sometimes they have needed a Saint Francis or a C. S. Lewis to remind them of the goodness of the natural world and the joyful pang of beauty.

Meanwhile, it is the duty of Christians today to care for the earth and to integrate this into their spirituality. Too long has it been a neglected aspect. As the Psalms praise God for the natural world (e.g., 104), and Jesus used natural parables (e.g., "Look at the birds," "Look at the flowers"), Christian appreciation for the work of God needs to be matched in our day by taking responsibility for life-style and economics in order to preserve the creation from human destruction.

We read in the Bible of a new heaven and a new earth, of a resurrection of the body and of the earth somehow giving birth to a redeemed creation (Rom. 8:19-25). These eschatological teachings are not a call to regard the earth with indifference, but to value it as God does, to prepare for the last day, whatever form the transformation takes, into a new existence in a renewed creation.

• DISCUSSION QUESTIONS

1. What are the most important images of God in your thinking? Do these images invite an intimate relation to God or create distance and silence?

2. How does naming God as Father, Mother, Friend, Healer, Rock, or Light help or hinder your relationship to God?

3. What could you do to show love to yourself? Is this approved by God or not? Why?

4. What basic teachings of the Bible encourage environmental responsibility? Why is Christianity held responsible by some people for the ecological desolation of the earth? What can churches and individuals do to make a difference?

• EXERCISES: Prayer and Pondering

Prayer is fundamental to Christian spirituality. Yet many people have difficulty with prayer because their training and experience have been too limited. Continuing childhood patterns, some adults always assume a posture of closed eyes, head bent, hands folded, and then list their requests to a God above the sky.

Prayer is freed up if one can pray at any time, any place, in any posture. Try praying while walking or running, driving the car or washing the dishes. Try raising your arms or opening your hands in a receptive way. Try singing and dancing. Not all of these will be helpful for every person, but the main point is to break out of cliches, to involve the body in prayer, and to integrate prayer into the duties of every day.

Devoting specific times for prayer each day is an important step toward the ideal of praying at all times.

1. Take time for silence as in chapter 1 to focus your attention and relax your body. Then deliberately raise your mind and heart to God. Become aware of God's presence, not somewhere above the ceiling, but indwelling you and all things. Spend some time without speaking to God but just being in God's presence. (How do you feel about this?) Then speak as you will.

It may be helpful to follow the acronymn ACTS: Adoration, Confession, Thanksgiving, Supplication. Adoration means praise and vocal love expressed to God. Confession means naming the things that keep you from loving and trusting God and receiving God's forgiveness. Thanksgiving may include the counting of one's blessings. Supplication is asking for help, either for oneself or for others.

There is no one right way to pray for all people, so do not get caught up in rigidly following the ACTS formula or any other. But it is important to attend to the various dimensions of prayer as indicated by these four letters, and perhaps to others. Prayer gets to be very dry when it is only S's (supplications).

If you do not pray much, it may be for a number of reasons. Perhaps a good spiritual counselor can best help you diagnose the problems. One of them may be anger at God that goes unrecognized because of teachings that suggest that it is wrong to be angry at God. God is big enough to handle our anger! God still loves us even when we tell God how angry we feel. Just as with a human friend, such telling can clear the air and revitalize the relationship. Some people will not admit anger, but rather withdraw from the person they are angry with and remain silent. This applies in the spiritual life when we withdraw from God and do not speak in prayer.

Prayer is communion with God and deserves a lifetime of learning. Do not let guilty feelings over past neglect prevent you from trying it anew.

2. *Lectio divina* is the practice of reading aloud in a slow, meditative way. Benedict's monastic rule emphasizes its importance. Choose a short passage of Scripture that stands out for you. Read aloud a psalm or a chapter from one of the Gospels. Stop when you come to a verse that seems especially meaningful. Then turn it over in your mind, seeking the ways in which it might encourage, convict, or liberate you. Use your imagination. Picture yourself with God or with other characters in the biblical story. Or, picture your own situation with a human character, Jesus, acting in it. Then listen and observe what happens.

• AIDS FOR THE EXERCISES

Bloom, Anthony. *Beginning to Pray.* New York: Paulist, 1970.

Hanson, Bradley. *Teach Us to Pray: Overcoming Obstacles to Daily Prayer.* Minneapolis: Augsburg, 1990.

Merton, Thomas. *Praying the Psalms.* Collegeville, Minn.. The Liturgical Press, 1956.

• SUGGESTED READING

Aaseng, Rolf E. *A Beginner's Guide to Studying the Bible.* Minneapolis: Augsburg, 1991.

Barclay, William. *Introducing the Bible.* Nashville: Abingdon, 1972.

Cummings, Charles. *Eco-Spirituality: Toward a Reverent Life.* New York: Paulist, 1991.

Koester, Craig R. *A Beginner's Guide to Reading the Bible.* Minneapolis: Augsburg, 1991.

Trobisch, Walter. "Love Yourself," in *Complete Works of Walter Trobisch.* Downers Grove, Ill.: InterVarsity Press, 1987. Pp. 653-92.

3 | The Beginnings of a Global Community

The first followers of Jesus were Jews, and Christianity became one sect, the "Nazareans," among others. But the beliefs of this sect—which saw Jesus as the Promised One, not only Messiah, but Suffering Servant, crucified for all and raised from the dead—led it to be rejected by other Jews, especially after the destruction of the Jerusalem temple in A.D. 70. Christians had largely escaped from Jerusalem and so did not share the suffering of other Jews. They also attributed the destruction to the rejection of the Messiah. This Jewish sect was excluded from synagogue worship by a curse on Christians inserted into the synagogue liturgy.

Thereafter, Judaism and Christianity separated, siblings created in the first century from the common stock of the people of Israel. The Judaism of today is the offspring of the rabbinic movement, which emerged fully about the same time as Christianity. Each group came to interpret the Hebrew Bible (the Old Testament) by means of a later collection of their own literature. The Jews used the Talmud, the Christians the New Testament.

The good news about Jesus came to be preached to Gentiles, especially those called "God-fearers," who were attracted to local Jewish synagogues but did not choose to be circumcised in order to become Jews. According to Acts, Paul preached to such people in his travels. Because of the Jewish rejection, the percentage of Jewish Christians dwindled, but Gentiles gladly heard this message, which included the monotheism and high ethical standards of Judaism without the requirement of circumcision.

What happened here was that Christianity emerged from being a sect within an ethnic group into a religion accessible to all peoples. Its roots were in Hebrew and Jewish culture, but now it became in principle transcultural, capable of expressing itself in a variety of cultures. In practice, the believers within the Roman Empire were from various ethnic cultures, largely overlaid by late Hellenistic (Greek) culture in the East and an emerging Latin culture in the West. Those outside Roman rule had other cultures, such as Coptic, Ethiopian, Celtic, or Persian, for example. The long-range implications were that Christianity was potentially a world religion, a faith that could interact with all human cultures. This interaction would later involve adaptations of both the practice of Christianity and the cultures it confronted, as the gospel message produced religious traditions of various types.

Gentile Christianity in the Roman Empire began as a minor sect that was frequently misunderstood and persecuted. In the first three centuries, the members were accused of atheism (not believing in any of the gods), cannibalism (eating the body and blood of Jesus in secret ceremonies), and superstition (believing what others did not believe because of an obscure Galilean preacher). Sometimes they were thrown to the lions or simply beheaded. By the time of Constantine, the first Roman emperor who claimed this faith, about 10 percent of the people in his empire had adopted Christianity as their personal faith.

In the years after 313, when Constantine declared Christianity a licit religion, the emperors came to embrace a church-state connection that was to be of great consequence for the history of Christianity in Europe and elsewhere. Constantine had founded a new city named after himself, Constantinople, to rule the later Roman Empire, now commonly called the Byzantine Empire. We know the city today as Istanbul, perched on the dividing line between Europe and Asia at the Bosphorus. By the fifth century, Christianity was no longer a persecuted sect, but a reigning majority, with wealth, status, and power.

That position of power was to prove a stumbling block to the growth of Christianity among non-European peoples, who began to associate it with the oppression of Byzantium. Within Europe itself, Christianity gained an imperial status it had not known during its first three hundred years of widespread growth. Now it expanded more frequently by royal edict than by personal conviction. Formerly it had been dangerous to be a Christian; now it was the socially accepted, or even the required, thing to do.

This transition meant that the hardy Christians of the first three centuries, especially the martyrs, were held in high regard by the privileged Christians of the next three centuries.

We see in the first six centuries the beginning and development of certain themes in Christian spirituality that are significant to the present day: worship and sacraments, charisms, witness unto death, spiritual disciplines, monasticism, and mysticism. These were important in both Roman and non-Roman contexts.

Worship and Sacraments Nourished
Early Christians

The individualistic assumptions we bring to spirituality did not apply in the first century. As Judaism developed a congregational form of worship in the synagogues of the diaspora, so Christians, the first of whom were Jews, assumed that public, communal worship was basic to spirituality. Those first Jewish Christians in Jerusalem, we are told in Acts, attended prayers in the impressive temple built by Herod the Great. But Christians in other places worshiped in the local house of prayer or synagogue.

Most of the basic elements of Christian worship were inherited from the synagogue: prayer, psalms, Scripture reading, sermons, and singing. What was added was the weekly meal of bread and wine, which seems to be an adaptation of the annual Jewish Passover or a rabbi's meal with his disciples, a *kiddush*. Partaking of this common meal, or Lord's Supper, was a celebration of the resurrection of the Master, who had said, "Do this in remembrance of me." But it was also seen as participating in the "body of Christ" and receiving this "bread of heaven" in a very realistic manner. This Eucharist ("thanksgiving") became the center of Christian worship.

First as small groups, later as immense congregations in cathedrals, Christians gathered on the first day of the week for prayer, preaching, and the Eucharist. Worship became more elaborate as time passed, but its importance for Christian spirituality was not questioned. Private prayer no doubt had its place, but the social character of the "body of Christ" meant that common prayer was central.

Baptism as initiation into the community was seen as the end of the old life and the beginning of the new. Some took this to signify that baptism meant the forgiveness of previous sins in the old life, but that the new life was to be perfect, without sin. This led to the postponement of baptism by some who feared that there would be no forgiveness afterward! Deathbed baptisms were not unknown, including the famous case of Constantine himself. The Roman preacher we know as Hermas had tried to dissolve this anxiety about baptism by writing in his book *The Shepherd* that there was indeed forgiveness for the baptized. It was not until ritual confession before the assembly was seen as a medicine for the postbaptismal sinner that people began once again to be baptized upon conversion or as infants.

Christian spirituality in the early centuries was communal spirituality, originating in baptism, rooted in the worship of the congregation, and nourished by weekly celebrations of the Supper instituted by Jesus.

Charisms Showed God's Love and Power

The "charismatic" element in Christianity refers to the gifts given to individual Christians for the common good. The Greek word for such a gracious, free gift, is *charisma*. These gifts may include very ordinary acts, such as washing someone's feet or sharing one's food, and extraordinary powers, such as instantly healing a sick person or conveying a specific message from God for a given situation. They are traceable to the earliest days of the church and are highlighted in both Acts and 1 Corinthians. The twentieth-century Pentecostal and charismatic movements look back to these roots as expressing essential elements of Christianity.

The book of Acts, probably written in the A.D. 80s, describes the earliest years of the church from the 30s to the 60s, from the departure of Jesus to Paul's arrival in Rome. This account emphasizes the role of the Holy Spirit in the development of the earliest church by describing the Pentecost event in chapter 2 and by continual references to the power of God's Spirit. This verse is often chosen as a summary of the book: "But you will receive power when the Holy Spirit has come upon you; and you will be my witnesses in Jerusalem, in all Judea and Samaria, and to the ends of the earth." (Acts 1:8)

It can be said that living the Christian life and developing the community are not within ordinary human ability. Only when the Spirit—in the fourth century described as the third person of the Trinity—empowers the disciples does the community grow.

In its "honeymoon" after Pentecost, the Jerusalem church lived a communal life, sharing goods. Later the church had more difficulty in overcoming ethnic differences in this sharing and appointed members of the deprived group who were "full of the Spirit and of wisdom" (Acts 6:3) to oversee the distribution.

Here are a few more examples of the work of the Spirit in Acts. In Acts 2 the Spirit is promised by Peter to those who repent and are baptized (v. 38). In chapter 4 the Spirit empowers Peter and the whole community to speak "the word of God with boldness" (v. 31). Chapters 7 and 8 describe how the Spirit guides Stephen and Philip. Paul, like all other major figures in the early community, is "filled with the Holy Spirit" in chapter 9 (v. 17). Finally, in chapter 10 we read how the first Gentiles received the Holy Spirit:

> While Peter was still speaking, the Holy Spirit fell upon all who heard the word. The circumcised believers who had come with Peter were astounded that the gift of the Holy Spirit had been poured out even on the Gentiles, for they heard them speaking in tongues and extolling God. Then Peter said, "Can anyone withhold the water for baptizing these people who have received the Holy Spirit just as we have?" So he ordered them to be baptized in the name of Jesus Christ. (vv. 44-48a)

The rather glowing picture of charisms, signs, and wonders in Acts must be compared with the more troubled picture that emerges from 1 Corinthians, written in the 50s. Paul writes to a church that is splitting, partly because of the spiritual pride of some who exercise charisms. He lists nine charisms in chapter 12, without saying that this is a complete list (compare Rom. 12:4-8 and Eph. 4:11-13):

> To each is given the manifestation of the Spirit for the common good. To one is given through the Spirit the utterance of wisdom, and to another the utterance of knowledge according to the same Spirit, to another faith by the same Spirit, to another gifts of healing by the one Spirit, to another the working of miracles, to another prophecy, to another the discernment of spirits, to another various kinds of tongues, to another the interpretation of tongues. All these are activated

by one and the same Spirit, who allots to each one individually just as the Spirit chooses. (1 Cor. 12:7-11)

It is clear that the church members in Corinth were misusing their gifts and thus tearing apart the community. In chapter 13 Paul inserts into his discussion of gifts the beautiful and profound hymn to love: "If I speak in the tongues of mortals and of angels, but do not have love. . . ." This chapter is much better known than his discussion of the charisms in chapters 12 and 14, but the context provided in the surrounding chapters helps us realize that he is talking about the gift of tongues.

Paul does not suggest love as an alternative gift to the others but as "a more excellent way" in which the gifts are to be evaluated and exercised. He underlines that the gifts are temporary, while faith, hope, and love are eternal. He emphasizes that love means patience, kindness, and humility in the exercise of the gifts.

Paul goes on to give specific instructions for worship services in chapter 14. He gives a very ambivalent account of speaking in tongues, which is described as praying with the spirit but not with the mind. On the one hand he asserts that this gift is very limited, since it edifies, or builds up, the one who prays in a tongue but is of no help to anyone else who does not understand it. He says that in church he would rather speak five words with his mind than ten thousand words in a tongue. He also suggests that not everyone speaks in tongues, and he urges Christians to seek the higher gifts, notably prophecy.

On the other hand, Paul affirms this gift, which seems to be the lowliest by his reckoning. He claims to speak in tongues more than any of them and says that it is not to be forbidden in the worship service. His implicit message is that speaking in tongues is best exercised in private prayer, where its edifying effect for the individual does not confuse other hearers.

It seems likely that many churches in the first and early second centuries practiced a spirituality that encouraged charismatic expression. The Syriac *Odes of Solomon* seem to come from Edessa or Antioch about the year A.D. 100 and express a charismatic spirituality full of praise and love for God.[1] The author(s) is unknown, but the odes may be a hymnbook, comparable to Psalms, that expresses a charismatic spirituality full of praise.

> As the work of the ploughman is the ploughshare,
> and the work of the helmsman is the steering of the ship,
> so also my work is the psalm of the Lord in His praises.
> My art and my service are in His praises,
> because His love has nourished my heart,
> and His fruits He poured unto my lips.
> For my love is the Lord;
> hence I shall sing unto Him.

For I am strengthened in his praises,
And I have faith in him.
I shall open my mouth,
and his spirit will speak through me
the praise of the Lord and his beauty. (16:1-5)[2]

Syriac Christianity used feminine symbols more frequently than did Greek
or Latin. The Holy Spirit was long identified as female, just as the Hebrew
word for spirit is feminine. A strong devotion to the Virgin Mary developed
early, including the legend that Mary bore Jesus without pain. This view seems
to romanticize the birth of Jesus instead of accepting the down-to-earth character of Mary and the Incarnation. Feminine images for God included the
breasts of God flowing with milk, a symbol of nourishment and delight. All
of these themes can be seen in the remarkable 19th Ode of Solomon, which
is worth quoting in full:

A cup of milk was offered to me,
and I drank it in the sweetness of the Lord's kindness.
The Son is the cup,
and the Father is he who was milked;
and the Holy Spirit is she who milked Him;
Because his breasts were full,
and it was undesirable that his milk should be released without purpose.
The Holy Spirit opened her bosom,
and mixed the milk of the two breasts of the Father.
Then she gave the mixture to the generation without their knowing,
and those who have received (it) are in the perfection of the right hand.
The womb of the Virgin took (it),
and she received conception and gave birth.
So the Virgin became a mother with great mercies.
And she labored and bore the Son but without pain,
because it did not occur without purpose.
And she did not seek a midwife,
because he caused her to give life.
She bore as a strong man with desire,
and she bore according to the manifestation,
and possessed with great power.
And she loved with salvation,
and guarded with kindness,
and declared with greatness.
                              Hallelujah.[3]

Following hints from the Old Testament, God is seen as female. Later,
several medieval mystics, men and women, would refer to God as Mother,
but retain the masculine pronoun, as here in the *Odes of Solomon*. See the
discussion of Julian of Norwich (pp. 65-66). The feminine images of God

are distinctive in Syriac spirituality; they are not necessarily a part of charismatic spirituality.

The charismatic phenomena of the first century seem largely to disappear in the following centuries. We have evidence concerning this change from a document, the *Didache,* or *Teaching of the Twelve Apostles,* commonly dated early in the second century. It is an anonymous writing, probably from Syria, that shows the structuring of the church out of the more fluid spontaneity of the charismatic period. Just as Paul dealt with problems concerning the use of tongues, this document warns about misuse of prophecy. It warns that traveling prophets should not be allowed to stay in a church for more than three days, lest they falsely fleece the flock.

Thus the sociological demands of better organization made it necessary for the leadership of the churches to become more learned and less spontaneous. Further, it seems from comments by the church fathers that they did not even know what speaking in tongues was; they had never heard or experienced it.

The Montanists, who were condemned as heretics, had a role to play in the growing disfavor of charismatic phenomena. Followers of **Montanus** (about A.D. 157) in Asia Minor emerged in the mid second century with a "new prophecy," an expectation of the Parousia, or return of Christ, and a rigorous set of ethical norms. They were led by Montanus himself and two female assistants, Maximilla and Priscilla. It was charged against them that they allowed women to speak and that Montanus claimed to be the Paraclete, or Counselor, promised by Jesus in the Gospel of John.

It seems likely that there was deliberate misunderstanding of their teaching. We have today almost no original writings that would give us their own spirituality; we have mainly the charges of their enemies. Much of what they taught was characteristic of the church in general a century earlier. They were not in step with the later replacement of the charisms by offices, easier rules of conduct, and waning of the imminent expectation of the Parousia. But the group itself moved in this direction by the third century. Tertullian, whom we will meet later in this chapter, became a Montanist at that time, but it was moral rigor that attracted him, not the exercise of charisms.

At any rate, these gifts continued to be practiced on the margins of the church until our own century, when they were rediscovered by Pentecostal and charismatic groups on all continents.

Martyrs Witnessed unto Death

In Christian tradition the martyr, man or woman, was honored for holding the faith as being of higher value than life itself, for showing what one ancient writer called "contempt" for the horrors of death. The root meaning of the word "martyr" is "witness," implying that death at the hands of Romans or others was fundamentally a testimony of faith. Our modern conception of a "martyr complex" suggests that the person who dies must be mentally unsound and that the ultimate value for any healthy person must be one's own life. Others, more thoughtful, see giving one's life as a testimony for truth as the ultimate gift of the truly healthy person.

Persecution of Christians began in the New Testament period, and it did not end until Constantine's legitimizing of the faith in 313. Jesus himself had said, "Take up your cross and follow me." During the sporadic persecutions by various Roman officials in different parts of the empire, the strength of conviction of Christians was severely tested.

The theme of martyrdom appears among the earliest group of writings after the New Testament, by the so-called Apostolic Fathers. Bishop **Ignatius of Antioch** (in Syria, Western Asia) (A.D. 160?-220?) writes on his journey to Rome, addressing letters to six churches and one bishop (Polycarp) along the way. Clearly his model is Paul, who is thought to have been martyred in Rome about A.D. 64. Ignatius's letters have the freshness and personal character of Paul's writing and often even the phrases of 1 Corinthians and other letters. There is a clear gap, however, between the apostle and his imitator. Ignatius's images, theology, and tone do not equal the depth of his mentor.

Ignatius describes his eagerness to die for his faith, asking readers to pray for his steadfastness. At the same time, he urges them to be unified and obedient to their own bishops and to avoid heresy, especially the teaching that Jesus did not really experience birth and death on a cross (Docetism).

"We have not only to be called Christians, but to *be* Christians," he writes to the Magnesians (4:1). For Ignatius, that clearly implies willingness to die for the sake of the faith. "If we do not willingly die in union with his Passion, we do not have his life in us" (5:1). It is in the letter to Rome that Ignatius most fervently expresses his desire for martyrdom, imploring his readers not to intercede and prevent his death. For Ignatius, death in the coliseum means that he will "get to God." This is his passionate desire, as the climax of his life on earth.

The world is mostly an enemy according to such a perspective. There is no time in these documents for meditating on the beauties of creation. Rather Ignatius exhorts his readers to fight the good fight, to be faithful to their bishops, and to avoid false teaching.

Another martyr in the early centuries was **Perpetua**, who met her death about A.D. 200 in Carthage. Much of the account of her martyrdom is first-person. As the young mother of an infant, she gave up her baby to others' care as she went to the stadium to meet wild beasts and eventually the sword. She defied the authority of Rome, not only to determine her religious practice, but even to choose the clothes in which she would meet her death. Her account of the last days, with a conclusion written perhaps by Tertullian, is one of the rare documents describing martyrdom as it was, and not in rhapsodic and legendary exaggerations.

Martyrdom stands as the ultimate test of any spirituality; it is the feature of discipleship that symbolizes the opposition of the world to Christian devotion as well as the utmost extent of Christian commitment. It indicates a testimony to one's faith that will not deny itself no matter what human society may do to enforce conformity. Martyrdom might be thought of as a passive act, allowing oneself to be killed. But clearly both Ignatius and Perpetua, though they were yielded to God's will, assertively refused to evade holy execution. In these cases, martyrdom is action in the world based on the example of Jesus himself.

Christians Practiced Asceticism

Certain disciplines have long characterized the Christian life. They involve exercise in virtue and avoidance of vice. Together these disciplines are called *ascesis,* or *asceticism,* words not often used favorably in our own age. The basic idea is that of athletic training in preparation for a contest, for example, a race. Paul writes: "Do you not know that in a race the runners all compete, but only one receives the prize? Run in such a way that you may win it. Athletes exercise self-control in all things; they do it to receive a perishable wreath, but we an imperishable one" (1 Cor. 9:24-25).

The Old Testament records not only a moral code, such as the Ten Commandments, but also special ascetic rules for certain situations, such as abstaining from food, alcohol, haircuts, or sex. In the New Testament, Jesus assumes that his followers will fast and give alms as was common in his own day (Matt. 6:1-4, 16-18). He speaks in dramatic metaphors about the seriousness of sexual lust (5:27-30). He calls on followers to deny themselves and take up the cross (16:24).

In the Hellenistic context, asceticism took on forms that seldom appeared within Judaism. The exaltation of virginity and the life of celibacy, for example, were sometimes motivated by views of the world that replaced the doctrine of creation with a world-weary, late Roman despair.

Indeed Paul had recommended celibacy in 1 Corinthians 7. He did so, however, because he believed the time was very short before the return of Christ and because women and men could devote themselves to the work to be done more wholeheartedly without a family. His discussion is surprisingly balanced in terms of men and women. For example, he sees each marriage partner having sexual desires and conjugal rights (vv. 2-3). But later writers urged celibacy for very different reasons, namely that the body is evil and sex is evil. Then the practice left behind the Jewish and Christian doctrines of creation, and the door was open for vilifying women as the object of the stifled sexual desire of celibate men.

Especially from the late-twentieth-century perspective, the practice of identifying women with sex and sin must be seen as very damaging to Christian spirituality. Asceticism was widespread in many cultures, not just Hellenistic ones, suggesting that it had a basic role in Christian spirituality but that it was misinterpreted or exaggerated in given situations.

Ascetic practices can be healthy or unhealthy. In a Christian context they need to meet two criteria for wholesomeness. First, do they affirm the goodness of creation? Is the motivation to free the person for better service, to give up something good for something better? If not, it may be a denial of the goodness of creation, of the body, sometimes of the goodness of sexuality.

The second criterion is whether the grace of God is being replaced by human effort. Is this effort being made in order to earn the love of God, which really cannot be earned because it is flowing toward us freely and unconditionally? Or is it a response to God's forgiving grace in Christ? Does the practice lead to the freedom of the athlete who runs in the knowledge of God's love, or to the bondage of a desperate attempt to earn what cannot be earned? Or is it perhaps self-punishment to atone for sins that Christ has already forgiven?

Three early Christian theologians who wrote in different languages nevertheless agreed on the importance of ascetic disciplines for the Christian life. Origen and Tertullian both were from Africa, and Ephrem was from Asia. Origen, who wrote in Greek, became head of a famous catechetical school in Alexandria, following his master Clement. Tertullian, a lawyer in Carthage (near today's Tunis), was among the first Christian writers to write in Latin. Because of their strong influence on the development of later Christianity, I will write at some length about these two men and then touch briefly on the Syriac writer Ephrem.

In **Tertullian** (160?-225) we hear the voice of the rigorist, one who exhorts the Christian to separation from the world. As a Catholic, before he turned to the rigor of the Montanist heresy, he wrote "To the Martyrs," "Spectacles," and "The Apparel of Women." Each of these ascetical writings demands separation from the pagan world of Carthage, North Africa, in about A.D. 200.

Tertullian tells the (potential) martyrs that they are better off in prison than in the world, since the world itself is a vast prison with disgusting moral rot and seductive temptations all about ("To the Martyrs," chap. 2). He argues with great dialectical skill against Christian attendance at the games and plays that are dedicated to pagan gods and exhibit no respect for human life or chaste morals ("Spectacles"). And finally he urges women to dress modestly, not in gold and make-up, as God did not intend it and there is no rational ground for such "lust" to please others. In these three essays (sermons) Tertullian makes clear that to him, a commitment to Christian spirituality meant a sharp break from "the world, the flesh and the devil" (the gods of the pagans).

Tertullian's discussion of pleasure in "Spectacles" (28, 29) (the general name for the various performances in Roman amphitheaters) is instructive.

There people were exposed naked for all to ogle, and blood-lust was encouraged by fights to the death.

> And finally, if you think that you are to pass this span of life in delights, why
> are you so ungrateful as not to be satisfied with so many and so exquisite
> pleasures given you by God, and not to recognize them? For what is more
> delightful than reconciliation with God, our Father and Lord, than the revelation
> of truth, the recognition of past errors, and pardon for such grievous sins of
> the past? What greater pleasure is there than distaste of pleasure itself, than
> contempt of all the world can give, than true liberty, than a pure conscience,
> than a contented life, than freedom from fear of death? To trample under foot
> the gods of the heathen, to drive out demons, to effect cures, to seek revelations,
> to live unto God—these are the pleasures, these are the spectacles of the Chris-
> tians, holy, everlasting, and free of charge.[4]

Tertullian does have a point, that Christians experience pleasures by virtue
of their faith and its practice.

But what is missing here is any sense of the small, daily pleasures of life—
looking at flowers, listening to music, making love with one's spouse, writing
creatively, laboring physically, and so on. To put it briefly, Tertullian has
missed the joys of the created order in his description of "Christian" pleasures.
Only the "spiritual" pleasures remain, as a foil to the artificial, often immoral
pleasures of the spectacles Rome provided for an increasingly callous
populace.

Tertullian laid the foundations for Latin doctrinal theology. As one of the
first Latin authors who had an intellectual grasp of the Christian message, he
forged new terms, such as *Old Testament, New Testament, Trinity,* and *person*
(to describe each member of the Trinity). His influence on Latin writers after
him was immense, and he was a major contributor to the eventual orthodox
view of the Trinity.

Tertullian rejected Greek philosophical influence in Christian theology. He
asked, "What does Athens have to do with Jerusalem?" His point was that
genuine teaching came from Christ, not from the speculations of the Gnostics,
who gained their inspiration from the Greek philosophers. In this regard he
was not influential, because for centuries much of the Christian theology of
the Roman Empire was a synthesis of Hebrew and Greek thought.

The good news does need contextualization, that is, expression within a
cultural context that is authentic to that culture. For example, Africans today
have the right and responsibility to think through the Christian message and
express its implications in words (preaching, theology, prayers) and artistic
expression (sculpture, dance, music) that is thoroughly African.

Tertullian's question, however, may be taken as a warning for all later
Christians. He calls for an evaluation of Christian teaching to see if it is true
to its sources or if it has been influenced by some other way of thinking that

distorts it. The tendency to ignore aspects of the message that challenge our assumptions is very strong when adapting the Christian message to one's own culture. Has the genuine gospel message been distorted by cultural adaptation? Have North Americans, for example, so interpreted the Christian message that it does not challenge their affluence in a world of poverty? In our day Tertullian might ask, "What does Madison Avenue have to do with Jerusalem?"

Tertullian eventually decided that even the Roman Catholic Church was not rigorous enough for him. He joined the Montanists, discussed above (p. 30), whose standards of behavior were even stricter than those of the Catholic church. He came to believe that there was no forgiveness of sin after baptism and that widows and widowers should not remarry. Tertullian's ascesis was sincere, consistent, and within the bounds of orthodoxy for much of his life. Yet he missed some very important themes in what we would consider a balanced ascesis, or spirituality, today. He missed the generosity of God in forgiveness, the wonder of the good creation, and the need for authentic contextualizing.

Origen (185-254), his younger contemporary, was intrigued by ideas, and is known as the first Christian "systematic theologian." That is, he sought to create a rationally satisfying system of thought that embodied Christian understandings of the world and God. He, like Tertullian, was eventually influential in the doctrine of the Trinity, but his approach was considerably different.

The days of the martyrs were far from over in Origen's time. His father was martyred in 203, and Origen himself wanted to offer his life to the authorities at age sixteen. Thanks be to his mother! She hid his clothes, and without trousers he was too embarrassed to go out of the house. One of the greatest Christian thinkers was saved for another day. Later Origen did in fact die from the effects of torture inflicted because of his faith, and he is rightly called a martyr.

Origen worked within the context of Hellenism, that is, Greek culture as spread by Alexander the Great and his successors. Origen lived in the intellectual center of Hellenism, in Alexandria (named for Alexander the Great). His question became, given the sort of worldview first developed by Plato and later developed by Plotinus (Neo-Platonism), how could one understand the Christian Scriptures?

Origen set himself the task of examining in great detail the Hebrew and Christian Scriptures. His *Hexapla* was an immense project, listing six different texts side by side for detailed comparison. Origen also wrote commentaries and preached homilies on much of the Bible. In spite of this biblical interest, Origen seems to have been controlled by his philosophical assumptions rather than by his biblical studies.

Origen postulated a fall of rational beings before the creation, which resulted
in human souls living in this world. That is, he thought that each person had
a preexistence, in which he or she somehow moved away from God. The
goal of human life is to return to God, and, in fact, Origen believed that all
humans would so return. These beliefs were among the most controversial,
leading to his later condemnation.

In 553, long after his death, Origen was condemned as a heretic. Yet
Origen's influence continued, especially through monks who found that his
spiritual teachings outweighed any questions about his orthodoxy in doctrine.
His spiritual teachings focused on martyrdom, prayer, and Scripture. He saw
the spiritual life as an ascent to God, much as the Hellenistic philosopher
Plotinus had envisioned it.

Origen set forth a three-stage schema for the Christian life, which in later
forms was to become normative for centuries to come. He spoke of moral,
natural, and contemplative levels. These are not totally exclusive or sequential
but nevertheless refer to stages of development. First, the moral level has to
do with behavior and can be compared to the book of Proverbs. Second, the
natural level is related to intellectual, observational activity, which is reflected
in Ecclesiastes. Finally, the contemplative level refers to the spiritual union
with God, exemplified in the Song of Songs (read allegorically, that is, as a
love song between God and the church).

Later the "purgative, illuminative, and unitive stages" of spiritual growth,
influenced by Neo-Platonism, would reflect this teaching of Origen. He influenced Gregory of Nyssa, who was a later theologian; Pseudo-Dionysius
(discussed later in this chapter, pp. 47-49); and much of Eastern and Western
monasticism.

The Latin and Greek languages used by Tertullian and Origen were not
the only forms of early Christian spiritual writing. Syriac, a later development
of Aramaic, the language of Jesus, was used in the Middle East, both within
the Roman Empire and east of its borders. It is a language much less familiar
to American scholars than Greek and Latin. Yet some of the important developments and documents of early Christianity are preserved for us only in
Syriac.

Syriac spirituality developed differently from that in cultures further west.
It is more closely related to Judaism, a Semitic culture, although sometimes
influenced by Hellenism. It became extremely ascetic. The anchorites (hermits) in the Syrian desert thought up bizarre ways to demonstrate their contempt
for comfort and the ways of the world. Most famous was Simon Stylites,
who lived on a pillar. Others found different ways, such as living in logs,
not bathing, and falling on their faces. Later writers tried to moderate the
extremes.

Of special interest is **Ephrem** (306?-373), whose works were copied long
after his death by Syrian monks. Ephrem expressed his teachings in symbolic

poetry that is still powerful today. He was a deacon in the town of Nisibis, on the border of the Roman Empire, today in southeastern Turkey. The last decade of his life was lived in exile after the victorious Persians insisted that all Christians leave Nisibis. He did much of his writing in Edessa, just west of Nisibis. One of the few events of his life of which we know is his service to victims of famine. In the last year of his life, he arranged for three hundred beds and food for the homeless and dying, personally serving their needs.

Ephrem advocated virginity, not because he despised the flesh, as some of the Greek writers seem to have done. Rather the grounds for his asceticism were marriage with the Bridegroom, the goal of wakefulness, and the ideals of Paradise.[5]

> The differences between these two approaches, Hellenic and Semitic, can be well illustrated if one visualizes a circle with a point in the center, where the point represents the object of theological enquiry; the philosophical tradition of theology will seek to define, to set *horoi*, "boundaries" or "definitions," to this central point, whereas St. Ephrem's Semitic approach through his poetry will provide a series of paradoxical statements situated as it were at opposite points on the circumference of the circle: the central point is left undefined, but something of its nature can be inferred by joining up the various points around the circumference. St. Ephrem is always very insistent that, since the center point representing the aspect of God's being under discusssion stands outside creation, it thus lies beyond the ability of the created intellect to comprehend—and any claim to be able to do so is blasphemous. In all this St. Ephrem is obviously very much in harmony with the apophatic tradition of later Greek theology.[6]

The learned Saint Basil had a great respect for Ephrem, and it is perhaps through Basil that the apophatic approach, which I will discuss later (pp. 48-49), became so influential. One point to notice here is that spirituality does not always follow from theology, but theology can follow from spirituality. Here is a sample of Ephrem's verse, in fuller expression of an apophatic approach to God.

> If someone concentrates his attention solely
>   on the metaphors used of God's majesty,
> he abuses and misrepresents that majesty,
>   and thus errs
> by means of those metaphors
>   with which God had clothed Himself for his benefit,
> and he is ungrateful to that Grace
>   which stooped low
> to the level of his childishness:
>   although it has nothing in common with him,
> yet Grace clothed itself in his likeness
>   in order to bring him to the likeness of itself.

Do not let your intellect
  be disturbed by mere names,
for Paradise has simply clothed itself
  in terms that are akin to you;
it is not because it is impoverished
  that it put on your imagery;
rather, your nature is far too weak to be able
  to attain to its greatness,
  and its beauties are much dimished
by being depicted in the pale colors
  with which you are familiar.[7]

Like many later theologians of the East, Ephrem saw the whole process of the Christian life as *theosis*, or divinization. This term was clearly expressed only once in the New Testament: "that you . . . may become participants of the divine nature" (2 Peter 1:4). But *theosis* was understood to underlie the New Testament message and became the basis for much Eastern spirituality. Here is a sample from Ephrem and a comment from Sebastian Brock, an expert on Syriac spirituality:

Divinity flew down and descended
to raise and draw up humanity.
The Son has made beautiful the servant's deformity,
and he has become a god, just as he desired.

It has sometimes been said that the concept of the divinization, or *theosis,* of humanity is something that crept into Christianity, and especially Eastern Christianity, under Hellenic influence. It is clear, however, that St. Ephrem, whom Theodoret described as "unacquainted with the language of the Greeks," and whose thought patterns are essentially Semitic and Biblical in character, is nonetheless an important witness to this teaching.[8]

I have discussed the asceticism of Tertullian, Origen, and Ephrem to show my conviction that asceticism is a valid aspect of Christian spirituality. However, it is sometimes based on a rejection of the fourth relationship in the model used in this book: our relation to creation. An extreme asceticism leads to despising God's good gifts of creation: our bodies and the world around us. A legalistic asceticism leads to despising God's grace in favor of personal merit. But a biblical asceticism leads to a healthy sense of being able to say no to a good thing for the sake of a better or higher one; it gives self-confidence while enabling people to serve others.

Monasticism Spread from Egypt

Africa was the scene of experiments in spiritual life that have shaped both the Western and Eastern traditions ever since. It was in Egypt that men and women first entered the desert to live out more fully the ascetical life they longed for, but the practice quickly spread to Asia and Europe. Among the first was **Antony** (about 250-353), whose life was described by **Athanasius** (296?-373), Bishop of Alexandria. Although Antony was a Copt, one of the peoples of ancient Egypt, and Athanasius was of Hellenist background, they came to know each other when Athanasius was exiled and ran for protection from the emperor's soldiers to the monks of the desert. Athanasius adhered stubbornly to the full divinity of Christ as stated in the Nicene Creed of 325. He suffered five exiles from opponents of the idea that Christ was of "One Being with the Father."

The Life of Antony tells the story of Antony's beginnings in the ascetical life after the death of his parents. He heard the gospel read in church, "Sell all that you have and give it to the poor." Immediately he did so. Renouncing economic power, he entered into training with others who knew this path, learning something from each one. A crucial step was Antony's dwelling in a tomb, the place of death, and overcoming everything that the powers of death could throw at him. Although nearly dead himself, he returned to the tomb from a "wake" in his own honor, to finally outlast the powers of the demons. The description of Antony's struggle in the tomb includes his rescue by Christ, who in Antony's experience (and in Athanasius's theology) was the victorious conqueror of death and demons.

Then Antony penetrated deeper and deeper into the desert, carrying his offensive to the opponents' "home territory." It was believed in Antony's time that the desert was the dwelling place of the devil and his minions. Recall that Jesus too had confronted Satan in the desert. Antony gave his whole time and energy to the struggle. Like other monks, he labored for his living, but he also spent time meditating on memorized Scripture. Many people came to him for advice and help.

Antony's life exhibits not only discipline but also tenderness and service. He not only lived the utterly simplified life of a hermit but also advised, reconciled, healed, and encouraged those who sought his aid. He did not so much escape from the world as engage the enemy of humankind in spiritual combat. Antony went forth in the power of the cross to defeat Satan through Christ's victory. In doing so, he forged a new style of Christian spiritual life, the monastic. He was not the first monk in the world, but he was among the very first who entered the far desert with specifically Christian motivations.

The sayings of many desert fathers and mothers (yes, women went out into the desert too!) have been collected and translated in many editions.[9] They have given insight into the sparse, clean, and rugged life of the desert, which has been a potent challenge and encouragement to all who seek a singleness of vision in our own day. Here are some samples of the short stories and words remembered from the Egyptian mothers:

[Amma (Mother) Theodora] also said, that neither asceticism, nor vigils nor any kind of suffering are able to save, only true humility can do that. There was an anchorite who was able to banish the demons; and he asked them, "What makes you go away? Is it fasting?" They replied, "We do not eat or drink." "Is it vigils?" They replied, "We do not sleep." "Is it separation from the world?" "We live in the deserts." "What power sends you away then?" They said, "Nothing can overcome us, but only humility." "Do you see how humility is victorious over the demons?"[10]

[Sarah] also said to the brothers, "It is I who am a man, you who are women."[11]

[Blessed Syncletica] also said, "If you find yourself in a monastery do not go to another place, for that will harm you a great deal. Just as the bird who abandons the eggs she was sitting on prevents them from hatching, so the monk or the nun grow cold and their faith dies, when they go from one place to another."[12]

She also said, "As long as we are in the monastery, obedience is preferable to asceticism. The one teaches pride, the other humility. . . ." Amma Syncletica said, "There are many who live in the mountains and behave as if they were in the town, and they are wasting their time. It is possible to be a solitary in one's mind while living in a crowd, and it is possible for one who is a solitary to live in the crowd of his own thoughts."[13]

The first experiments with communal monasticism, as opposed to the individual or anchorite type practiced by Antony, were accomplished by Pachomius, also in the Egyptian desert. But the most influential founders of this type of monasticism were Basil of Caesarea in the East, the Greek-speaking half of the Mediterranean basin, and Benedict of Nursia in the West, the Latin-speaking part of the empire, increasingly centered in Rome.

In the East, from what is today Turkey, **Basil of Caesarea** (330-379) was a major influence on monasticism. A strong belief in the superiority of communal monasticism led Basil to write two monastic rules. His emphases were on the whole of life as thanksgiving, on the spiritual gifts, and on the importance of obedience in attacking self-will. The whole process of growth, or sanctification, is the process of restoring the image of God, lost by the first parents. Basil defended Trinitarian doctrine, just as Athanasius before him. He was influential in asserting the full divinity of the Holy Spirit and the final acceptance of the Nicene Creed at Constantinople in 381.

However, he was also influenced by the earlier Alexandrian, Origen, and he selected some of Origen's writings for the original collection of spiritual writings named the *Philokalia* (the love of beauty, parallel to "philosophy," the love of wisdom). Later we will discuss another, much larger *Philokalia* collected in the eighteenth century. Basil's own spiritual teaching, unlike that of Origen, leads from light into divine darkness, rather than from darkness into divine light. This surprising reversal is more fully developed by Pseudo-Dionysius, whom we will study at the end of this chapter.

Basil had two associates who worked with him: Gregory of Nyssa (his brother) and Gregory of Nazianzus (his friend). Together the three are known as the Cappadocian fathers, after the region of Cappadocia in Asia Minor. All shared a commitment to the Nicene Creed, but each had different gifts. Basil was the organizer, the bishop, the abbot. Gregory of Nyssa was the most gifted intellectually. And Gregory of Nazianzus was most eloquent. Macrina, Basil and Gregory of Nyssa's sister, influenced them very much.[14]

Evagrius of Pontus (345?-399) is an important link between the Cappadocians and later writers, especially monks, Eastern and Western. He knew the Cappadocians personally, but he also traveled to Egypt and lived in the desert there. His teaching was influenced most strongly by Origen and to a lesser degree by Gregory of Nazianzus, and he became a Christian Platonist, following the lines of the philosophy developed by Plato. Though he was later condemned with Origen, his teachings circulated anonymously or under pseudonyms. It is striking that heretical writers were so influential in medieval Christian spirituality.

The goal of life, according to Evagrius, is the recovery of the knowledge of God and the unity of rational spirits, lost in the primordial fall. The Christian life has "stages": the practical, natural, and theological. Evagrius analyzed the dangers to the Christian life to be eight in number. These were later pared down to seven by John Cassian and became the "seven deadly sins." Evagrius's list included gluttony, lust, avarice, dejection, anger, despondency (*akedia*, or "accidie"), vainglory, and pride.[15]

Apatheia (passionlessness or freedom from passion) was for Evagrius the healthy functioning of the soul's powers. It was the desirable state for Christians but not the only goal of Christian living. He thought that the goal of prayer was a stripping of the mind, a pure consciousness of God without images or thoughts. This would restore the lost knowledge of God.

John Cassian (about 360-432) took Evagrius's teachings to the West. He knew Evagrius in Egypt, then traveled to Marseilles, where he founded a monastery. He wrote a number of books, including his *Conferences*, which reflected what he had learned from the Egyptian monks, especially Evagrius. These readings were canonized by Benedict for reading by monks and thus came to be commonly accepted in the West. The ideas were basically those of Evagrius but are now in the context of Gaul and in the Latin language. John Cassian was a cross-cultural transmitter of the ideals of the Origenist stream of Egyptian monasticism.

In Italy, **Benedict** (about 480-547) founded the Benedictine Order, still one of the largest Catholic religious communities. After experiments with solitude, he came to develop a system of monastic governance that gave the abbot a great deal of authority while insisting on mutual discussion and advice. His *Rule* is relatively brief and nonlegalistic: the basic principles are set down without trying to settle all cases in advance.

One of the fundamental spiritual principles of the *Rule* is the incorporation of physical labor with prayer. The motto is *Ora et Labora*. The rhythm of prayers seven times each day interspersed with physical labor and eating and sleeping in moderation, became the norm for Western monks up to the present day.

Benedict also prescribed *lectio divina*, or sacred reading, for four hours each day (see the exercise at the end of chapter 2). Monks were to read the Scriptures and the early Christian writers and then meditate on them in silence or while working (six hours daily). He praised silence as a virtue. How far we have come from his ideals today, with constant noise and little time to concentrate, think, and meditate, even in church!

The vows taken by monks and nuns in succeeding centuries are not defined in Benedict's *Rule,* but they do reflect his influence. Vows of poverty, chastity, and obedience are intended as forms of spiritual discipline that make possible a life of community. Poverty by choice is a way of loosening the bonds of possessions that Jesus had warned about. Chastity, in this case, celibacy (not having sexual intimacy with anyone), was intended to loose one from sexual bonding for community service. Obedience is perhaps the hardest of these disciplines and the one most emphasized by Benedict, for it implies bending the will to another, namely the abbot. This humble renunciation of one's own will to another human being was intended to show the submission of the Christian to God. It is clear that the abbot carried a heavy responsibility in Benedict's plan.

The founding Christian in **Celtic tradition** is Saint Patrick (389?-461?), who was able to convert the women powerful in Celtic society and to found monasteries all over Ireland. The Celts, a people who had moved from central Europe to settle in Ireland, Scotland, Wales, and western France, were outside the Roman Empire. They developed a distinctive culture and religion led by druids. Patrick, who had been a slave in Ireland, returned as a missionary. We have very little exact knowledge of Patrick, but many legends survive. The following *lorica* (breastplate) is attributed to him.

> I arise today
>   through God's strength to pilot me:
>   God's might to uphold me,
>   God's wisdom to guide me,
>   God's eye to look before me,
>   God's ear to hear me,
>   God's word to speak for me,
>   God's hand to guard me,
>   God's way to lie before me,
>   God's shield to protect me,
>   God's host to secure me
>   against snares of devils,
>   against temptations of vices,
>   against inclinations of nature,

against everyone who shall wish me ill,
afar and anear,
alone and in a crowd.[16]

From the start, monasticism was important to Celtic adherents of the new faith. There was direct influence from the Coptic monks of Egypt, and *The Life of Antony* was well known. The church was headed by abbots rather than bishops. "Double" monasteries, for both women and men, were common and were sometimes headed by a woman. The most famous of the women saints of Ireland, Brigid, was such an abbess.

Irish Christians lifted the concept of the *anamchara,* or "soul friend," to importance in their spirituality.[17] One was not alone in the Christian walk, but the close companion could encourage and correct one along the way. This was a relationship for counsel, confession, and support, which finds biblical precedent in the words of James in the New Testament. "Therefore confess your sins to one another, and pray for one another, so that you may be healed" (James 5:16).

Like Syriac monasticism, the religious in Ireland were extremely strict in their asceticism. The practice of reciting all 150 Psalms daily was common, and some stood praying in icy water. They spoke of white martyrdom, the daily ascetic practice; red martyrdom, the shedding of blood; and blue martyrdom, the doing of significant penance for sin.

A distinctive feature of Celtic spirituality, which later spread to all Roman Catholicism, was the practice of private confession with fixed penances for given offenses. Confessional books called *penitentials* prescribed the penance to be paid for a given sin. Later when Irish monks converted many Germanic peoples on the continent, this practice was extended to them.

After the Lateran Council of 1215, it became a required practice in Catholic churches to confess to a priest. Later, at the Council of Trent in the mid 1500s, Penance was defined as one of the seven sacraments. This sacrament was amended after Vatican II in our own century to eliminate the quantitative approach that had become characteristic and to give more freedom of practice. Today the renamed Sacrament of Reconciliation is probably closer to the original Celtic practice than was the enumerating of sins in the confessional characteristic of the period from Trent to Vatican II.

Another distinctive form of asceticism was self-exile from one's home or monastery. It came to be common for Irish monks to leave home as Abraham had been called to do and live far from the community that had nurtured them. This traveling led indirectly to the spread of Christianity in northern Europe.

Among the exiles was Saint Columba, who landed on the Scottish island of Iona in 632. He is said to have slaughtered five thousand men and wished to do penance by saving as many among the pagan Scots. Iona became a mission station and may have been the location of the illustrating of one of the most beautiful manuscripts ever copied: the *Book of Kells*. This illustrated biblical masterpiece was taken back home to Ireland for safety from the Viking attack.

Today Iona is the home of an ecumenical Christian community founded in the 1930s that emphasizes Christian living in one's calling, including prayer, meditation, and social service. Pilgrims such as I travel to Iona for retreats in the restored Abbey, amid Celtic crosses that predate the Viking era.

Another example of the importance of Christian monasticism was in the area we now know as **Ethiopia.** Christianity had been declared the religion of the kingdom of Axum (or Aksum) in the fourth century. This occurred because two students traveling from Tyre to India were shipwrecked on the Red Sea coast near the capital. The king put them in charge of educating his children, and around A.D. 330 King Ezana became a Christian. One of those students, Frumentius, was named the first bishop. He was consecrated by Athanasius in Alexandria. From that time until 1951 the abuna, or chief bishop, was named by the Coptic bishop in Alexandria.

But the evangelization of the people of Ethiopia was not accomplished by the king. This task was carried out by the Nine Saints, each from a different country, who arrived in 480 and spread the faith through monastic houses. They set about the huge task of translating the Bible into the Ge'ez language, one of the oldest biblical translations. They also translated *The Life of Antony* and the *Rule* of Pachomius. In fact, these saints had lived in Pachomius's monastery before coming to Ethiopia.

The Ethiopian church grew and developed in contact with the Byzantine churches until the Arab conquest of the seventh century. Then it was shut off from Red Sea trade, became isolated, and moved inland within present-day Ethiopia.

Today members of the Ethiopian Orthodox Church are expected to fast many days in the year and to pray seven times daily. Prayer is commonly said while standing, with complete prostrations at the beginning and end. The *debteras* or choristers sing at joyful festivals while dancing solemnly with long sticks. Some of these practices may go all the way back to the ancient monks who founded Ethiopian Christianity.

Mysticism Developed in East and West

Mysticism is a term much used and misused. The reader must always ask in what sense the term is used in order to understand the writer's meaning. The word comes from ancient Greek religion, and its root meaning is "secret." The participants in rites of the Greek pantheon were not to divulge the proceedings to outsiders. Eventually everything mysterious was connected with "mysticism."

The term is an elastic one, used by different writers in different ways. In general, mysticism is a form of spirituality that sets as its goal unity with

God (or, in some religions, with the "Ultimate"). Mystics generally have reached a level of contemplation at which they cannot describe their experiences and so use colorful language and poetry to convey the gist of it to those who have not experienced their ecstasy. They tend to see the whole world as charged with divine glory, and they sometimes change the world by their vision of justice and love.

The essential meaning of mysticism in the Christian tradition is the experience of God as one with whom one has union or communion. The last two terms are extremely important. Union with God can mean complete absorption, ultimately losing one's identity in God. It can be argued that such a view goes against the grain of orthodox Christian teaching, for it suggests that ultimately there is no self, and therefore redemption and moral responsibility become null and void. If there is no redeemed person, then Christianity loses its basic view of the world.

Communion, on the other hand, suggests a kind of loving relationship of two persons who remain distinct in spite of a unity of purpose, feeling, and/ or knowledge. Christian mystics have had a great deal of difficulty articulating their experiences of God, and most have spoken of union with God. Whether the term is to be understood in an absolute sense, as above, or in the modified sense of communion, must be determined in each individual case.

Two of the most influential writers of the early period wrote in a mystical vein. They came from opposite ends of the empire, and their teachings were in very different modes. They are Augustine of Hippo in North Africa and "Dionysius the Areopagite," probably from Syria.

Augustine (354-430), the celebrated author of *The Confessions,* gave a narrative character to Christian growth that had not been present before. It was a brand-new concept: a book that narrates one's inner life with God. Augustine addresses God throughout the book, confessing both sin and faith. He tells his story in a conversation with God that leads him to appreciate God's love for him every step of the way.

In reconstructing his past, Augustine was searching out the ways God had been seeking him, and he found that what happened was not entirely in his own power. The sense of being in the hands of forces greater than oneself is very strong, and the narrative character of the understanding brings down to earth some of the principles and proverbs of the Egyptian monks. The story of Antony of Egypt is what led to Augustine's final break with his old life and his turning to a new one.

The whole of *The Confessions* testifies to a personal longing for God finally satisfied. Tracing his early years, Augustine tells of his mother Monica, a devout Christian who became the most influential person in his life, and his father Patricius, a non-Christian. He recalls his unhappiness in school, his attraction to Manichaeism, a religion teaching that the matter of the world is an evil opponent to the good spiritual God, and his departure from Manichaeism. Having become a teacher of rhetoric, Augustine seeks his fortune in Rome and Milan. There he finds the framework for all his subsequent thought in late forms of Plato's philosophy and is convinced by the preaching of Bishop Ambrose that one does not have to commit intellectual suicide to believe the Bible.

Finally, in a famous scene in a garden, he gives up the struggle and gives in to God. Hearing children nearby singing, "Take up and read," he reads from Romans 13:13-14, "Let us live honorably as in the day, not in reveling and drunkenness, not in debauchery and licentiousness, not in quarreling and jealousy. Instead, put on the Lord Jesus Christ, and make no provision for the flesh, to gratify its desires."

Since Augustine had been living with a concubine, this verse seemed pointed at him. His sexual life with her had been the glue that first kept him from becoming a Christian. Now, on his conversion it was thoroughly repudiated. We do not know what became of the concubine whom Augustine sent away, but from that time on, Augustine was never able to enjoy a conscience-free sexual relationship. His view of women and of sexual intercourse was never very positive after conversion.

Augustine later connected sexual desire with a biological transmitter of "original sin," the sin inherited after Adam and Eve's first disobedience. It was the parents' sexual lust that made every birth impure. For Augustine the starting point of Christianity thus became the fallen nature of humanity, the grace of God restoring that fall by means of Jesus' death on the cross, mediated through the sacraments. His views came to dominate later Catholic and Protestant thought, which will be contrasted below with the Eastern perspective of *theosis* and resurrection.

After his baptism Augustine decided to return from Italy to North Africa, where he was born. On the way, in Ostia, he and his mother shared an experience of union with God. They ascended in conversation until they in silence "slightly touched" Wisdom.

Finally, after his mother's death, he returned to Africa. And because of his intellectual superiority, he was forcibly ordained a priest and later a bishop. In Hippo he established a monastic community around the cathedral and entered a long career of writing and church administration.

In his conflict with **Pelagius** Augustine championed the grace of God against human effort as the means of salvation. Pelagius, a contemporary of Augustine, reacted against the weak-kneed mediocrity of Christians in Britain, his home, who gave up the moral battles of the Christian life by saying, "I can't do it. If God wanted me to, God would give me the strength." Relying on grace and not on human effort seemed a cop-out to Pelagius.

This issue is fundamental to Christian spirituality and was the prime reason for the later split in the church between Catholics and Protestants. How are we to understand the role of God as Savior and the human being as actor in the Christian life? Augustine was convinced that any good thing in his life was a gift of God, not his own achievement. He had been rescued from his old life not by his own efforts, but by the love of God. If he had been able to save himself, there would have been no purpose in Jesus' death and resurrection.

In the long run, the Catholic church sided with Augustine in its synod and council decisions, but in parishes the role of the human will in "working out one's salvation" was often more prominent. Later the Protestants would appeal to the anti-Pelagian writings to support their teaching of "grace alone."

Augustine also wrote treatises arguing against the Donatists, strict adherents of a purification movement among the Berber Christians to the south of his area. They were inheritors of the cult of martyrs, including Perpetua, and of the rigorist attitude of Tertullian. Augustine declared that baptisms performed by unworthy priests were still valid, whereas the Donatists accused clergy of deceiving the soldiers during persecution and refused to receive their sacramental acts. Augustine became embroiled in a battle not only of words but of force, endorsing the use of soldiers against the Donatists. The split in the North African church was part of the reason that the church disappeared there after the Arab conquest in the seventh century.

In conclusion, Augustine left a mixed legacy for the Latin-speaking church. He was an intellectual who bound together the Platonist philosophical tradition with the biblical faith, emphasizing the Psalms and Paul. He was a synthesizer who combined the basic insights of the Greek and Latin writers of the first four centuries into an orthodox vision of truth. He was a sojourner who gave new expression to the personal walk from carnality to a loving God with whom he sought union. He was a teacher whose bad conscience, unhealthy sexuality, and emphasis on original sin left a legacy of gloom and misogyny on much of Western spirituality. But for all his faults, Augustine's final word was adoration of the grace of God.

The second figure who stands at the roots of later Christian mysticism is an anonymous writer known to later centuries as **Dionysius the Areopagite.** It seems that a Syrian monk of about the year 500 wrote under the name of Dionysius in order to claim the authority that comes from the apostolic age, for nothing is known of the original Dionysius except his name in Acts 17:34. This writer is commonly known therefore as Pseudo-Dionysius.

Four books have come down to us under this author's name: *The Celestial Hierarchy, The Ecclesiastical Hierarchy, The Divine Names,* and *The Mystical Theology.*

Among his major contributions are the formulation of the three stages later to become standard in all Western mysticism—the purgative, illuminative, and unitive. There were previous triads, but Pseudo-Dionysius was the first to name them in this way. *Purgative* refers to a period of cleansing, *illuminative* to the light of God shining on the soul, and *unitive* to the experience of oneness with God.

The influence of Neo-Platonism, a later form of Plato's philosophy, is very strong in the conception of the spiritual life in Pseudo-Dionysius. Much of his thought is parallel to that of Proclus, a contemporary non-Christian philosopher. Yet he has distinctly combined Christian understandings of God with the philosophical framework.

He operates with a worldview that is triadic and hierarchical. In fact, he invented the word *hierarchy* in Greek. Everything in the universe is seen to be in threes, with carefully described levels from top to bottom. He does not seem as interested in the relationship of Father, Son, and Spirit as with the notion of threeness, which he sees at all levels of the hierarchy.

One of the most powerful and distinctive teachings of Pseudo-Dionysius is his apophatic theology, which means a theology beyond words and images. He believes that since all human concepts limit and distance God, they must be stripped away from the mind if God is to be known. He begins his discussion of *The Divine Names* by echoing Paul in Romans 11 on the inscrutable nature of God. "Indeed the inscrutable One is out of the reach of every rational process. Nor can any words come up to the inexpressible Good, this One, this Source of all unity, this supra-existent Being. Mind beyond mind, word beyond speech, it is gathered up by no discourse, by no intuition, by no name."[18]

Then in *The Mystical Theology* Pseudo-Dionysius introduces the theme of divine darkness, of the need to strip away the intellect in the knowledge of God. He begins with poetry, which is a forerunner of Saint John of the Cross, whom we will meet in chapter 5.

Trinity! Higher than any being,
  any divinity, any goodness!
Guide of Christians
  in the wisdom of heaven!
Lead us up beyond unknowing and light,
  up to the farthest, highest peak
  of mystic scripture,
  where the mysteries of God's Word
  lie simple, absolute and unchangeable
  in the brilliant darkness of a hidden silence.
Amid the deepest shadow
  they pour overwhelming light
  on what is most manifest.
Amid the wholly unsensed and unseen
  they completely fill our sightless minds
  with treasures beyond all beauty.

[Reader,] . . . leave behind you everything perceived and understood, every-thing perceptible and understandable, all that is not and all that is, and with your understanding laid aside, to strive upward as much as you can toward union with him who is beyond all being and knowledge. By an undivided and absolute abandonment of yourself and everything, shedding all and freed from all, you will be uplifted to the ray of the divine shadow which is above everything that is.[19]

Pseudo-Dionysius argued that since any human concept is inadequate for God, only denials of the likeness of God to human categories could properly apply. For example, it would limit God to say, "God is just" (in the positive). It would be better to say, "God is not unjust" (in the negative). He asserts, however, after a long list of such negations, that God is even beyond denial.

The process of stripping one's concepts of God of all that is unworthy is called the *via negativa,* or the negative way. It is the intellectual side of apophatic theology. One of the striking features of the writings of Pseudo-Dionysius is the combination of a highly intellectual discussion of God with an absolute denial of the power of the intellect to know God.

The affective side of apophatic theology is a spirituality that requires a state of utter passivity on the part of the mystic. According to Pseudo-Dionysius, such passivity leads to an ecstasy of love in which the human is fused with God. This theme is to be seen in a great deal of later mysticism, for example, in Meister Eckhart, whom we will meet later (pp. 62-63).

The opposite of apophatic is kataphatic, which means an active attempt to image God by the use of one's imagination and emotions. The practice of meditation by means of calling forth images from the Scriptures, for example, is kataphatic. Pseudo-Dionysius clearly thinks that the kataphatic way has its utility, notably for beginners on the spiritual way. But for those approaching union, the apophatic way is necessary.

We conclude by noting again that Christianity in the early centuries de-veloped in a number of cultures and was expressed somewhat differently in each of them. The foundational developments occurred not only in Greek and Latin contexts, but in Syriac and other lesser-known contexts. The same themes we have discussed here—worship and sacraments, charisms, martyrdom, asceticism, monasticism, and mysticism—appeared in Ethiopia and Britain, India and Syria. It is clear, however, that the Greco-Roman synthesis was the dominant form in number and wealth.

- ## DISCUSSION QUESTIONS

1. Why were early Christians so devoted to ascetic practices? Is this a feature that we in the twentieth century need to delete from Christianity? Or are the practices of asceticism necessary to Christian spirituality? Do traditional forms of asceticism need to be changed in order to show that Christianity can affirm the human body?

2. What do you see as the strengths and weaknesses of the monastic tradition? Is it important to have religious orders of celibate men and women? Do you see value in having some part of the Christian community devote itself entirely to prayer, or is this an unhealthy spirituality?

3. There have been more Christian martyrs in the twentieth century than in any other. Under what circumstances is someone to be called a Christian martyr (witness)? What is the difference between a genuine martyr and someone with a "martyr complex"?

4. Do you find yourself more attracted to the apophatic or the kataphatic way of relating to God? Why? What can you learn from the other position that may be helpful for your spirituality?

• EXERCISES: Communal Worship and Fasting

1. "Going to church" may be very significant for your personal spirituality or it may be irrelevant, depending on what you make of it. The Christian walk is not ideally a private walk; it means being part of a people, an organic "body of Christ" that extends down through the centuries and over all continents. The local community of faith you choose is an expression of that "body." It should be a place where you are known, accepted, loved, challenged, and made accountable. The worship experiences you share will be focused on word and sacrament. Hearing the law and gospel preached is important for one's growth, as is receiving the Lord's Supper (sometimes called the Eucharist, Holy Communion, or mass).

Be intentional about your church attendance. Do not simply go through the motions. If you are attending a church that does not provide a meaningful worship experience, then try to change things. Or perhaps a different congregation or even denomination can better meet your need. One cannot simply sit back and expect a congregation to serve the individual; churches are places to give service, not simply to be "spiritually entertained." But it is a good idea to visit a number of different church traditions to see the variety of ways in which God is worshiped. A balance of intellect and emotion is needed, according to different needs.

Before attending a church service, take time to meditate about your intentions. Seek the presence of God and a genuine meeting with the people. Have a prayerful attitude during the service, with an open ear. When you sing a hymn, really praise God through it. On some occasions that praise will be more precious than any other part of the service. On other days the bread and wine of the Eucharist will be most meaningful. The preacher may speak just the word you need on other occasions. It is not often that all of these things will happen in one service, so it takes a kind of patience to be in a Christian worshiping community. Some days our hearts are cold, the sermon is boring, and no one makes contact with us. On other days the music and the Spirit invade our hearts.

2. An ascetic practice usually goes against the grain. It exercises the power to say no to a familiar practice. Care must be taken to recognize the goodness of something one will do without for a limited period of time.

One of the oldest types of self-denial is fasting. I recommend that any healthy person can find value in fasting, but it should be done with good guidance and moderately to start. It is very important to take in enough fluids. (Remember the first paragraph of this book!) Fasting may not prove immediately helpful. Try it a few times to find the pattern that best fits you. Partial fasts may be more helpful than complete fasts. Fasting is not a good way to try to lose weight, but when done properly, it can indeed bring into focus the real values of life. A sense of interdependence with others and dependence on God can result from fasting. It is also wise to use the time normally devoted to eating to the practice of spiritual discipline such as prayer or reading. Fasting can increase one's sense of freedom and strength. One discovers, "I can *choose* to eat or not to eat."

• AIDS FOR THE EXERCISES

Beall, James Lee. *The Adventure of Fasting: A Practical Guide*. Old Tappan, N.J.: Revell, 1974.

Foster, Richard J. "Fasting," "Confession," "Worship," "Guidance," and "Celebration" in *Celebration of Discipline: The Path to Spiritual Growth*. Rev. ed. San Francisco: Harper, 1988. Pp. 47-61, 125-71.

Kiefert, Patrick R. *Welcoming the Stranger: A Public Theology of Worship and Evangelism*. Minneapolis: Fortress, 1992.

• SUGGESTED READING

Brock, Sebastian, trans. *The Syriac Fathers on Prayer and the Spiritual Life*. Kalamazoo, Mich.: Cistercian, 1987.

Colliander, Tito. *Way of the Ascetics: The Ancient Tradition of Discipline and Inner Growth*. San Francisco: Harper, 1982 (1960).

Ephrem the Syrian. *Hymns*. Classics of Western Spirituality Series. Translated by Kathleen E. McVey. New York: Paulist, 1989.

Lawrence, C. H. *Medieval Monasticism*. 2d ed. New York: Longman, 1989.

O'Donoghue, Noel Dermot, O.D.C. *Aristocracy of Soul: Patrick of Ireland*. Wilmington, Del.: Michael Glazier, 1987.

4 | The European Era

In this chapter, I will discuss Christian spirituality from about the fifth to the fifteenth centuries. I have called the chapter "The European Era," because Christianity had lost ground geographically in Asia and Africa but had spread to new cultures in northern Europe, notably to the Anglo-Saxons, the Germans, the Scandinavians, the Ukrainians, and the Russians. The development of spirituality in these new areas was to be significant for world history in centuries to follow.

It was a period of gradual separation of the Greek East from the Latin West, where "East" and "West" assume the Mediterranean Sea as the center of the earth. The East centers in Constantinople and the West in Rome. The usual date of separation of the Roman Catholic and Eastern Orthodox churches is 1054, but there were many ups and downs in this relationship from about 800 to 1200. The Fourth Crusade (1202) finally left bitterness beyond measure when Roman Catholics sacked the Eastern capital, Constantinople. This was a period in which the Dark Ages were followed by high scholasticism, a period of many attempted reforms in the Western church.

The East

In the early centuries, the differences between East and West were cultural, but the church had an overall unity of spirit, if no single leader or pope. The various ancient cities of the apostles, Jerusalem, Antioch, Ephesus, Alexandria, Rome, and later Constantinople, each had a patriarch. But the patriarch of Rome, the only patriarch in the West, gradually claimed unique authority over the others. They did not agree to be ruled by him, and tensions mounted.

Drawing on the traditions of Greek theology and the ecumenical councils up to 787, the Eastern church came to have distinctive emphases that differed from the West. The "ecumenical" councils were those representing the whole "inhabited world." This is the same word used in the twentieth century for the movement to unify the churches of different denominations. The church was not divided into denominations at that time, so representatives from the Roman East and West participated at Nicea in 325, Constantinople in 381, Ephesus in 431, Chalcedon in 451, Constantinople (II) in 553, Constantinople

(III) in 680-681, and Nicea (II) in 787. After this, the Roman Catholic Church continued to call councils, but they were not recognized by the Eastern Orthodox.

In the areas near the Mediterranean the Eastern Church lived under Islamic rule after the seventh century and was pressured to stop any evangelism or outward Christian display. In 1453 the unthinkable happened: the very center of Byzantine rule fell to the Muslim Turks, and the great cathedral Haggia Sophia became a mosque. No longer named Constantinople, the city has since been called Istanbul.

In the areas where missionaries had taken the new faith, notably Ukraine and Russia, Christianity came to be associated with the rulers as it had in Byzantine days, so Moscow counted itself the "Third Rome," center of a Christian empire after the fall of Rome and Constantinople.

Eastern theology was strongly Trinitarian, firmly based on the early councils, the Holy Tradition. It saw the spiritual development of the Christian in the schema of divinization or *theosis*, the process of humans becoming divine.

The Jesus Prayer: The Prayer of the Heart

The fundamental idea of the Jesus Prayer is to pray constantly. This requires a kind of attention to God that becomes habitual while one goes about the tasks of daily life. The prayer is a short formula that is repeated constantly in rhythm with one's breathing or heartbeat. After a period of learning, the prayer repeats itself naturally without conscious effort. It is sometimes called "the prayer of the heart."

Today the most common form of the prayer is "Lord Jesus Christ, have mercy on me." But the emergence of the prayer was gradual. Different forms of words and different understandings of their function can be seen in the fifth to eight centuries. Kallistos Ware, a present-day scholar and bishop of the Orthodox Church writes that there were four elements that eventually came together in this prayer:

1. Devotion to the Holy Name *Jesus*, which is felt to act in a semi-sacramental way as a source of power and grace.
2. The appeal for divine mercy, accompanied by a keen sense of compunction and inward grief (*penthos*).
3. The discipline of frequent repetition.
4. The quest for inner silence or stillness (*hesuchia*), that is to say, for imageless, nondiscursive prayer.[1]

The roots of the Jesus Prayer lie in Scripture. The publican prayed, "God, be merciful to me, a sinner!" (Luke 18:13). Paul exhorted, "Pray without ceasing" (1 Thess. 5:17). And Peter preached, "This man is standing before

you in good health by the name of Jesus Christ of Nazareth. . . . There is
no other name under heaven given among mortals by which we must be
saved" (Acts 4:10, 12).

Some elements of the prayer can be found in the Desert Fathers and Mothers,
but it developed distinctively later with Diadochus (fifth century), who was
influenced by Evagrius in seeking "prayer without thoughts"—that is, without
images or words—and gave a practical method for seeking it (see 4 above).
But he was also influenced by Macarius in an affective emphasis, valuing
experience and not just intellect.

It may be surprising for us today that the Jesus Prayer was further developed
in Gaza and Sinai, areas of recent Middle East conflict, by monks with names
such as Barsanuphius, John, Dorotheus, Philemon, John Climacus, Hesychius,
and Philotheus. The Sinai writers may hint at the connection between the
recitation of the prayer and the rhythm of breathing, which became explicit
in the Middle Ages.

In the Middle Ages the prayer became widely used among Orthodox monks.
Much later, in the late nineteenth century, the anonymous *Way of a Pilgrim*
took the prayer to the West from Russia. Ware says that it is used in the
twentieth century by more Christians, East and West, than in any century
before. He clarifies its practice by writing:

> By modern Western writers it is sometimes termed a "Christian mantra," but
> this could give rise to confusion. The Jesus Prayer is not simply a rhythmic
> incantation, but an invocation addressed directly to the person of Jesus Christ,
> and it presupposes conscious, active faith in him as only-begotten Son of God
> and unique Saviour. It is not, however, a form of discursive meditation upon
> particular incidents in Christ's life, but has as its aim to bring us to the level
> of *hesuchia* or stillness—to a state of intuitive, non-discursive awareness in
> which we no longer form pictures in our mind's eye or analyze concepts with
> our reasoning brain, but feel and know the Lord's immediate presence in a direct
> personal encounter.[2]

From this apophatic practice we turn to one that is also distinctively Eastern
but emphatically kataphatic: the use of icons in worship. The apophatic moves
beyond images; the kataphatic employs images.

Icons Were Windows to Heaven

The visual representation of the human form in a certain style came to be a
distinctive spiritual and theological expression of Orthodox Christianity. Icons,
it is claimed by the Orthodox, were present even in the time of the apostles,
and were an intrinsic part of the Christian message from the beginning. We
might expect, however, that only after the time of Constantine, when the

churches had a stable existence, large buildings, and financial resources, did the golden paintings we know today begin to emerge.

The status of icons was clarified in the eighth and ninth centuries during the Iconoclastic Controversies. These were theological and political disputes within Eastern Orthodoxy. The major theological issue behind the conflict was the nature of the incarnation. Did the Word of God really become flesh, really enter the material world in Jesus of Nazareth? If so, as the doctrinal tradition claimed, then what were the implications for the nature of Christian worship? Was the adoration of God to be purely mental, or did images and human art have an important role to play?

Iconoclasts, those who wanted to throw the paintings out of the church, argued that it was unworthy of God to be represented and venerated in a physical object. The veneration of paintings and statues appeared as idolatry from this point of view. Some of the emperors in Constantinople used their power to physically destroy icons.

Defenders of such representation and veneration replied that this practice was consistent with the mystery of the incarnation. It was taking seriously the human nature of Jesus, the goodness of creation, and the sacramental quality of all things, for it implied that a physical object could be the meeting place between God and human beings.

The seventh ccumenical council in 787 approved the use of icons, stating, "The honor rendered to the image passes to its prototype, and the person who venerates an icon venerates the person (*hypostasis*) represented in it."[3]

Thus one of the most distinctive features of all Eastern Orthodox Christianity was preserved. Today as then, the human figures in the icons are seen as windows on eternity, as means by which worshipers may participate in the divine. Eastern Orthodox spirituality continues a devotion to Jesus; his mother, the "Theotokos" or Bearer of God; and all the saints, by means of lighting candles and incense before icons and kissing them. Family and private worship also include this practice, for many Orthodox homes have a special worship center with icons.

In our time worship with icons could be called "right brain" prayer, using images rather than discursive language. It is one kataphatic approach in the Eastern tradition, along with elaborate liturgical gestures and architectural symbolism in churches. The apophatic approach is also present in the East, as seen, for example, in the Jesus Prayer. These need not exclude each other, but both can be practiced to complement each other.

Gregory Palamas Defended Hesychasm

Hesychia (or *hesuchia*), stillness or silence, is the word for a prime tradition in Eastern spirituality. It refers to going apart to the desert for solitude. Its greatest theologian and defender was **Gregory Palamas** (1296-1359), a monk of the famous group of monasteries at Athos in Greece, archbishop of Thessalonika, and writer of many theological volumes.

Typical of the Eastern tradition, Gregory saw the goal of the Christian life in the statement of Athanasius, "God became man so that man might become God."[4] That is, the major axis of the faith is not human sin and divine redemption on the cross, but rather human mortality and divine victory in the Resurrection. The incarnation of God in Jesus was the way in which God defeated the powers of death and sin through the passion, death, and resurrection of Jesus.

Gregory and the other monks on Athos, experiencing a spiritual revival there, were attacked by an Eastern theologian of Western training named Barlaam. It was he who caused Gregory to break his silence and defend in his writings many of the distinctive characteristics of Eastern spirituality. Notably, Gregory approved of trying new methods, even if some should later be found wanting, in seeking union with God, which is the process of divinization or *theosis*.

As a theologian, Gregory made the important distinction between the Energies of God, which humans may know, and the Essence of God, which they cannot know. He defended the possibility of a vision of God in this life, even before death, though it is not perfect. He defended various extreme physical disciplines used with the Jesus Prayer. Thus Palamas disagreed with Barlaam, urging the importance of the body and its postures in prayer.

Gregory stated that the union with God is essentially by God's grace, yet the vision of God in this life could not be attained without hard work, and was easier for solitary monks than for the married. There is a cooperation or synergy between the divine grace and human will: Those who search with all their hearts for unceasing prayer will be given the gift of prayer (a gift of grace). The gift of tears (a constant flow of joyful tears) will be given to those whose passion for things of earth is being transformed into passion for things of heaven. Unlike some earlier writers, Gregory sees positive passions as well as negative ones. Thus for him "passionlessness" (*apatheia*), or freedom from destructive passions, does not refer to a denial of the body, but the transformation of body and soul together.

For Gregory Palamas, the transfiguration of Jesus was the revelatory event that showed the present and future kingdom of God. The glory of God and of Christ was visible to the three disciples as a sign of the actual presence of the kingdom. That kingdom is still present for those given the gift of seeing it, but it will be perfected for those who after death see God face to face.

The West

As the East in this period was characterized by icons, the Jesus Prayer, and hesychasm, in the context of a monastic church spreading northward, the

Western church also spread north, developing new forms of religious orders and mysticism.

Western Europe focused more on sin as the enemy of humankind and on the cross of Jesus as its solution, as compared with the Eastern focus on death as the enemy and the resurrection of the Christ as the victory of God.

Monasticism Was Renewed by Spiritual Leaders

Among the great medieval spiritual teachers is **Anselm of Canterbury** (1033-1109). He is known for his contributions to systematic theology (his teaching of atonement by satisfaction of God's justice) and to philosophical theology (his ontological argument for the existence of God). His life of deep piety produced these writings, which became a bridge between the early writers and the Middle Ages. His theme phrase came originally from Augustine: "I believe so that I may understand, and what is more I believe that unless I do believe, I shall not understand."[5]

Anselm wrote *Prayers and Meditations* to help others pray. The book shows his commitment to thoughtful meditation, the combination of rigorous intellectual work and devotion to God in Christ.

Within the Western tradition, no one was greater in the twelfth century than **Bernard of Clairvaux** (1090-1153). He was known for reform of the monastic tradition, returning to the simplicity of the *Rule* of Saint Benedict, and eventually administering a vast network of monasteries. In his public life he preached to recruit participants in the Second Crusade in 1146, and in later life he had so much power that he was the virtual pope of the Western church. Our brief survey cannot recount the story of this dramatic and troubled series of events.

Bernard was declared a doctor of the Roman Catholic Church by Pope Pius XII in 1953. The encyclical declaring this honor is called *Doctor Mellifluus* (or the doctor-flowing-with-honey) because of the sweetness of his teaching compared with the dryness or harshness of some other medieval writers. Indeed his teaching, focusing as it does on love, is both positive and personal, but not sentimental, as the title may suggest.[6]

In his teaching on the spiritual life, Bernard focuses most clearly on the relationship between the self and God. Borrowing a good deal from Augustine, Bernard, in his treatise "On Loving God," sets forth four degrees of this love. He sees the self first of all loving only itself, then loving the neighbor and God for its own sake. Third, the soul comes to love God for God's sake, normally the highest plane of love. But there is a fourth level, in which the soul loves itself for God's sake. This is found only fleetingly on earth but will be the constant state of the dead after the resurrection of the body.[7]

Bernard emphasizes the importance of the human Jesus for Christian spirituality. He refers more frequently than his immediate predecessors to the New

Testament portrait of Jesus, not merely as an example of a holy life, but as the divine action of love to change the hearts of human beings. Bernard's sermons on Advent and Christmas rise to the heights of praise for the incarnation.

His *Sermons on the Song of Songs* are a striking example of "spiritual" interpretation of the Bible. The eighty-six discourses cover only the first two chapters of the Song, but the most striking feature to a modern reader is the breathtaking reversal of the sensuous, erotic metaphors of the poems to an appeal against the passions of the flesh, and a description of the joys of spiritual intimacy with God. Here the Bridegroom is Jesus, and the Bride, the soul of the Christian. "What a close and intimate relation this grace produces between the Divine Word and the soul, and what confidence follows from that intimacy, you may well imagine. I believe that a soul in such condition may say without fear, 'My Beloved is mine. . . .' "[8]

Writers in our time have suggested that the roles be reversed and that God or Jesus become the female partner. The passionate nature of God's love is emphasized here, suggesting a divine *eros* for humanity, in contrast to the dispassionate *agape* as it has been interpreted by some Protestant writers.[9] Eros suggests the kind of longing experienced by lovers, whereas agape has been portrayed as the love of the unlovable, a determination of the will to seek what is good for the one loved. Both words are needed, in my opinion, to convey the richness of God's love.

Bernard emphasized the role of humility in the Christian life, for example, in his comments on the Song of Songs. The knowledge essential for the Christian is knowledge of the self and of God. Such self-knowledge is humility. He says, "There is no danger, however much you may humble yourself, that you will regard yourself as much less than you really are—that is to say, than truth holds you to be."[10]

In the light of modern psychology, many of us would demur at this point and argue that a healthy regard for one's worth before God can enhance rather than retard the loving relationship. Or, to put it another way, Bernard has looked at one particular danger to the relationship to God, that of arrogant pride, but he has not seen the opposite danger, such low self-regard that the soul cannot enter a relationship with the divine. This too might be a perverse form of pride.

A movement to revive the ideals of twelfth-century monasticism was begun by Gerard Groote in late fourteenth-century Netherlands. It came to be called the "modern devotion" (Devotio Moderna), not really because it was something new, but because it sought to develop a devotion to Christ that was as characteristic of life outside the cloister as within it. The movement developed into a monastic order, a subgroup of the Augustinians called the Windesheim Congregation, but also to a group of over one hundred houses in Holland and Germany of the **Sisters of the Common Life and the Brothers of the**

Common Life. These disturbed some people because they had all the appearances of a new monastic order but without permission. The members practiced poverty, celibacy, and obedience but never took formal vows. Their daily life was very much like that of Benedictines.

What was distinctive in the Sisters and the Brothers was a spirituality that focused on the imitation of Christ. This theme, which became the title of the best-known book of spirituality throughout western Europe, demanded that disciples of Jesus follow the way of the cross. Knowledge of the self and denial of the self, together with contempt for the world, are enjoined on the reader. The probable author is **Thomas à Kempis** (1380-1471), one of half a dozen major leaders in this movement. The book breathes a strong eucharistic piety as well as the practice of constant meditation, not only during quiet times, but in the midst of work.

The "Modern Devotion" differs from the best of twelfth-century spirituality by seeing no value in the intellectual life. The intricacies of scholasticism and the immoral lives of some monks who claimed to be learned had convinced its members that true knowledge does not come from books but from the identification of one's life with God, the fusion of knower and known. One of the famous paragraphs in *The Imitation of Christ* reads:

> What good does it do to speak learnedly about the Trinity if lacking humility you displease the Trinity? Indeed it is not learning that makes man holy and just, but a virtuous life makes him pleasing to God. I would rather feel contrition than know how to define it. What would it profit us to know the whole Bible by heart and the principles of all the philosophers if we live without grace and the love of God? Vanity of vanities, all is vanity except to have God and serve him alone.[11]

This view was to influence Protestant Pietism in later centuries. It is a good reminder that theology calls for an appropriate life as well as intellectual tools; spirituality is part of theology. But it can also lead to despising one of God's good gifts, the human intellect.

Mendicant Orders Emerged as a New Form
of Religious Life

The thirteenth century was a time of important developments for Christian spirituality and theology. It is commonly regarded as the peak of the "high" Middle Ages, that is, the time of fruition and fullest development in this period of history.

Among the dramatic events was the founding of mendicant (begging) orders, a new development in the history of monasticism. The Dominicans, the Franciscans, the Carmelites, and the Augustinians exemplified a new understanding of the necessity of meeting the needs of the church and the society. Instead of binding themselves to stay in one monastery, there to engage in communal and private prayer, these new orders called for service in the world as the first priority. To varying degrees they retained monasteries (now "houses"), common prayer, and direction by an abbot (now a prior). All continued the basic vows of poverty, chastity, and obedience, but the practice of these vows was adapted to new circumstances.

Dominic Guzman (1170?-1221) saw the need for better preaching in the Roman Catholic Church. Heretics in southern France were making inroads on an uneducated laity; the typical and damaging response of rulers was to put the heretics down by military might. Dominic had experienced some success in persuasion rather than force. He founded an Order of Preachers, commonly called Dominicans, who could speak to the people with knowledge and effectiveness. Very soon this order became one of the best educated groups in Europe, and its spirituality focused on the piety of learning.

Studying and preaching came to have even more value for this order than poverty or obedience. Mendicancy (begging for one's living) was eventually abandoned as impractical, and obedience was in tension with the understanding that the preacher was independent and that the rule of the order was a human instrument, not a divine law. The order retained a great deal of flexibility and developed one of the most adaptable systems of governance, which was later copied by many subsequent orders.

The Dominicans helped produce some of the greatest scholars in the history of Europe, namely Albert the Great (c. 1200-80) and his student **Thomas Aquinas** (1225-74). Thomas was later the most influential theologian in the Roman Catholic Church, having incorporated the philosophical perspectives of Aristotle into the theological tradition he inherited from Augustine and many others.

Thomas viewed the Christian life as a colloquy or friendship between humans and God, emphasizing the role of charity as the measure of all vows, practices, and steps. It is said that Thomas himself left off on his great *Summa Theologica* for the sake of a life of prayer and meditation. All he had written was but as straw compared with the wonders he experienced in a mystical unity with God.

It was another Dominican, Alan de La Roche, who in the late fifteenth century introduced one of the most popular and enduring features of Catholic piety: the rosary. The rosary is a physical aid to prayer and meditation, consisting of 150 beads, usually formed into a circle with a crucifix attached. Praying the rosary is a way of both repeating familiar prayers (the Our Father, the Hail Mary, and the Doxology) and meditating on sacred "mysteries," that is, important events in the lives of Mary and Jesus. There are five Joyful Mysteries relating to the birth of Jesus, five Sorrowful Mysteries concerning the suffering of Jesus, and five Glorious Mysteries recounting the resurrection of Jesus and the honoring of Mary. These fifteen mysteries are recalled in concert with the 150 beads.

Thus the mind operates on two levels: the repetition is simply a way of centering the attention, while the mysteries are imaginatively relived. Obviously this devotion depends on the belief that Mary, together with all the saints, is able to hear the prayers of the faithful and is an appropriate mediator to her son Jesus and to God. Most Protestants have not been willing to accept these beliefs, but a few in our own day are advocating the use of the rosary by Protestants. Roman Catholics have made the rosary less prominent since the Second Vatican Council, especially in public worship.

The second great founder of a mendicant order, and surely one of the most fascinating and challenging figures of the whole medieval period is **Francis of Assisi** (c. 1181/2-1226), founder of the Franciscan Order, or the Friars Minor (little brothers). His life is associated also with **Clare of Assisi** (1193-1253), the founder of the Second Order for women, or the Poor Clares. It is difficult to write briefly about figures whose lives have attracted so much attention, so many legends, so many analyses.

Francis has been called the saint who most clearly exemplifies the life of his Savior, with whose love he was enflamed. It began when a young, enthusiastic, worldly youth heard the call of the gospel passage in which Jesus sent out his disciples to preach in Galilee. Francis was given love for lepers and the desire to "rebuild" the church. He fell in love with "Lady Poverty" and wandered as a mendicant, praying, preaching, and helping. He found freedom from possessions so exhilarating that he determined to own nothing of his own. Soon others were attracted by his joy and simplicity, and the band of twelve was approved as the Order of Friars Minor

Later Francis was forced to compose a rule for the rapidly expanding order. He was never known as a gifted administrator, but rather as a free spirit. He visited the Holy Land and preached to the Muslim Saracens, and in 1224 retired to pray on Mount La Verna. There he received the answer to his prayer for identification with the Savior; the stigmata of Christ, the wounds of the crucified Jesus, appeared in Francis's flesh.

It was after this, in his last two years of life, that he wrote his well-known *Canticle to the Sun*, in which he addresses all things in creation as his brothers and sisters. Even death in this poem becomes a sibling of the singer, in a sharp reversal of the attitude of Paul and others who saw death as an enemy.

Francis, writing about the sun and moon, the fire and air, as siblings, is one of the few outstanding spiritual writers to make the fourth relationship of our model, the relation to the creation, a major part of his message. The legends of Francis and the wolf and Francis preaching to the birds extend his simple theme of the Fatherhood of God to all creatures, not just to humans. The humility and the joy expressed in this man encompass both identification with the pains of the crucified Jesus and the happy and carefree humility that trusted the Father of birds and flowers to provide his needs.

Clare, a woman of Assisi who had observed Francis for some time, asked to become a member of his band. She became the leader of the Second Order for women, whose life was more traditionally monastic; the sisters did not wander from place to place as the men did. For her, poverty was the door to contemplation of the Jesus who was himself poor and served the poor.

A Third (Franciscan) Order for lay people was added later and became a powerful stimulant to Christian life for those not called to the life of the religious orders.

The men's order developed with much internal strife after the initial bands had expanded and the influence of the magnetic personality of Francis no longer personally influenced the new members. Greater or lesser strictness concerning poverty was the debating point for centuries to come.

One of the greatest Franciscans was Saint Bonaventure (1217-74), who was minister general of the order. He integrated his great learning of the classics with the influence of Francis in a large number of writings.

Mysticism Came to a New Flowering

Women and men who gave themselves to a life of prayer and meditation in the late Middle Ages are commonly called mystics. At times mysticism became faddish, and there was a great deal of phony pretension and seeking after supernatural phenomena. The mature mystics always warned against seeking flashy effects in favor of seeking God alone.

One can distinguish two basic kinds of mystics, those who were more affective (focused on the affections) and those who were more intellectual and philosophical. The former type included many whose writings have been called "Bride-mysticism" because of concentration on the images from Song of Songs relating to marriage to Christ the Bridegroom. Bernard of Clairvaux fits this description.

Of the latter type, the most outstanding example is **Meister Eckhart** (1260?-1328?), a Dominican who influenced John Tauler (1300?-61) and many other influential preachers and writers. His vague expressions in his German sermons led to considerable confusion as to his exact meaning. Near the end of his life some of his Franciscan enemies brought charges against him, and a number of his statements were condemned as heretical. He was accused of heresies related to Neo-Platonism: pantheism (the view that God is the world and the world is God), making no distinction between God and the soul in mystical union, and the denial of God's freedom in creation. The validity of these condemnations is still hotly debated by the adherents of "creation spirituality" (see p. 119). They contend that Eckhart was a biblical preacher. He was influenced by Celtic and Eastern Christianity and served communities of women called Beguines. These women were not wealthy enough to have a dowry for entrance into a monastery, so they lived according to their own rule in the world. The Beguine movement began in 1223 in the Rhine Valley but was condemned about a century later by Pope John XXII.[12] Eckhart was influenced by these women and especially by Mechtild of Magdeburg.

An important issue is how much Eckhart is to be seen as a Neo-Platonist author and how much a biblical one. It seems that Pseudo-Dionysius was a very strong influence, especially on Eckhart's doctrine of God.

Many women and men could be chosen for discussion in this section. Among them are Hildegard of Bingen (1109-79), an abbess on the Rhine who included visual art in the reports of her visions; Mechtild of Magdeburg (d. 1300?); Joachim of Fiore (c. 1135-1202), who developed a distinctive apocalyptic spirituality; Henry Suso (c. 1295-1366), another Dominican follower of Eckhart; Catherine of Siena (c. 1347-80), whose concern for reform of the church led to direct influence on the Pope; Catherine of Genoa (1447-1510), called the "Theologian of Purgatory"; and Walter Hilton (d. 1396), Richard Rolle (c. 1300-49), and the unknown author of *The Cloud of Unknowing*, all English mystics of the fourteenth century.

I have chosen two mystics for closer attention, Jan van Ruysbroeck and Julian of Norwich. The first of these, **Jan van Ruysbroeck** (1293-1381), though not widely known, is highly regarded by students of mysticism because he drew together the two major strands of mysticism, the affective and the intellectual. He shows the influence of Pseudo-Dionysius, Augustine, Bernard of Clairvaux, and Meister Eckhart. After serving for twenty-six years as a secular priest, Ruysbroeck and three other mystics withdrew to a forest priory near Brussels. He composed his major works there in vernacular Flemish.

In *The Spiritual Espousals* Ruysbroeck uses and modifies the traditional three-stage schema of mystical growth, (1) the purgative, (2) the illuminative, and (3) the unitive. The most important change is his repeated insistence that the stages do not follow one after the other, but are added on. Thus the first is included in the second, the first and second in the third. These three differ from the traditional arrangement also by including true union with God already in the second stage, though intermittently.

Ruysbroeck calls his stages (1) the active life; (2) the interior, or yearning life; and (3) the God-seeing, or contemplative life. In *The Sparkling Stone* wayfarers on these steps are named respectively the faithful servants, the secret friends, and the hidden sons of God.

1. The spiritual life begins with conversion. The person uses free will to turn to God and begin the way back to God. Such a turning is empowered by grace and results in charity. This turning then leads to the cleansing of conscience through contrition, penance, and dislike of oneself. One is truly in the active life when by means of the light of grace, a will turned to God, and a clean conscience, the spiritual eyes are opened. One enters a life of virtue and service to others.

2. To this life of exterior works the second stage adds the practice of interior exercises. In this stage the imagination must be purged of all creaturely images, all clinging to the world, that the soul may be prepared for God. Whereas in the first stage one's union with God was achieved through grace and works and sacraments, in the second stage one begins to know union with God without such means.

3. In the third stage the union with God which the yearner has known in the second stage becomes of a higher and more permanent quality. Whereas the person was characterized by a seeking and a great hunger, he or she is now at rest, in "fruition" or "delectation." Yet one who has attained this "fruition" lives an active life also. This highest life Ruysbroeck calls "common." It is life in both contemplation and service, given to all people in common as God gives to all in common.

These stages of union with God are accompanied by a unification of the self as well. Likewise, though to a lesser degree, the wayfarer is united to other people. Using one of his favorite metaphors, fluid, Ruysbroeck explains how one is melted by the heat of the Holy Spirit and flows out to all types of persons.

Holiness in unity means the discarding of multiplicity or at least of all things opposed to one's union with the One. Intellectually, this means approaching God with a bare mind, aware that "where understanding remains without, desire and love enter within."[13] It means entering the divine darkness, having removed creaturely images from the mind.

Volitionally it means abandoning one's will to God's will. This involves aligning all of one's affections Godward, not clinging to anything in the world. And finally it means dying to oneself, "melting" and flowing into God. Whereas the "friends of God" (those in stage 2) "retain something of their own self, and so are not consumed and burnt to naught in the unity of love," "the sons [in stage 3] experience a simple, deathlike passing over into a state devoid of form."[14] In the highest stage "All our powers then fail us and we fall down in open contemplation. All become one and one becomes all in the loving embrace of the threefold Unity. When we experience this Unity, we become one being, one life, and one blessedness with God."[15]

Ruysbroeck, like many other mystics, is not always easy to read. Although his work is clearly organized, he warns the reader, "Here you must pay careful attention, for anyone who has never experienced this will not easily understand it."[16]

In spite of his many words, Ruysbroeck usually has a light and joyful tone. He is far from morbid, always pointing to joy, peace, rest, and enjoyment in God. Though he indicates an awareness of sin, it remains on the periphery of his vision; he focuses on God and on the blessings of union with God.

Ruysbroeck instructs the reader in an objective tone, never directly speaking of himself. He will speak of "man" even when it seems he is indirectly referring to his own experience. His description of "spiritual drunkenness," which must reflect some of his own experience, is one of the most memorable paragraphs in the *Spiritual Espousals*. His basic approach is not to say "this is what I have seen" as does Julian of Norwich (see below), but rather "this is what may be seen." He maps the terrain of the spirit, which includes highly subjective features, in an objective tone.

As we look at Ruysbroeck's writings, we see a focus on the relationship between the self and God as primary, with some attention to the self's relation to itself and to others. Union with God is the dominant theme; unification of the self is corollary. The relationship to creation seems to be a negative one. According to Ruysbroeck, the world even in the positive sense of creation is a hindrance to union with God and plays no positive role in Christian spirituality.

Julian of Norwich (1353-1416?), for long centuries unknown, has come into prominence in the late twentieth century. Most of what we know about her is from a single book in two versions, a Short Text and a Long Text, commonly known as *Revelations of Divine Love*. She tells us that when she was thirty and a half years old she not only was on the point of death, but she received an answer to prayer that she should share in the sufferings of Christ on the cross. In fact, she was given sixteen visions or "showings," which far exceeded the extent of her prayer. They were recorded soon afterward in the Short Text.

Julian of Norwich spent the next twenty years pondering and praying over these showings, as the Long Text indicates. In the meantime she had become an anchoress, a woman who lived a solitary life in a small cell attached to the church of Saint Julian in Norwich. So little do we know of biographical detail that we do not even know her name but only the name of the church we use to identify her.

Julian's writing was informed by knowledge of Paul's letters and the Gospel of John. She also knew the main ideas of Augustine, yet she regarded herself as unlettered. Perhaps she did not know Latin, but this, the first book in English known to be written by a woman, shows remarkable learning.

It is easy to contrast Julian's writing with that of her contemporary Margery Kempe, whose autobiography tells how she went to consult Julian. Margery's spiritual life was characterized by copious tears, loud groans, and erotic images, which made most of her male acquaintances very uneasy! Margery writes that she found her visit with Julian comforting and reassuring, which does not surprise the reader of Julian's book.

Julian is also known for writing of Jesus as our Mother. She did not invent the image, since other spiritual writers had drawn upon it before her. But she uses it in a more theologically knowledgeable way than her predecessors. It is not just that mother love is an illustration of Jesus' love for us, she says, but the very nature of his relation to us is explained by it.[17]

In contrast to Ruysbroeck, Julian is not interested in mapping out the mystical landscape, in discussing the stages of the Way, or even in giving rules for the moral life. Rather, she is setting out carefully, intellectually, the conclusions of years of pondering her showings. She is more interested in enquiring into the mysteries of God, humanity, sin, and redemption than in charting her own spiritual progress or that of others. Thus she is known today as a theologian, not simply a visionary.

Julian's dominating question is how to understand the presence of sin in a world created good by a good Creator. She does not answer the question in discursive theology, but by pondering the images and narrative of one of her showings. In this showing, the lord sends his servant on an important errand, but the servant falls into a pit. The master looks on him "with pity, not with blame." This fall is taken to be both the fall of Adam into sin and the self-emptying of Christ in becoming human. In the end, Julian says, sin was "behovely," or necessary, for the fullness of God's plan to send Christ and to rouse humanity to love. She concludes with a beautiful passage showing that the underlying theme of the whole is the love of God.

> And from the time that it was revealed, I desired many times to know in what was our Lord's meaning. And fifteen years after and more, I was answered in spiritual understanding, and it was said: What, do you wish to know your Lord's meaning in this thing? Know it well, love was his meaning. Who reveals it to you? Love. What did he reveal to you? Love. Why does he reveal it to you? For love.[18]

There is an eschatological dimension in Julian's vision that is often lacking in mystical writers. That is, she looks forward to the consummation of all things. The world may be a small hazelnut in a human hand, but it is precious to God, and God will redeem it. We do not get the sense in Julian that the world is only a shell, to be thrown away like garbage for the sake of human souls, but that just as Paul writes in Romans 8, the creation will share in the redemption of the children of God. Her statement quoted and made famous by T. S. Eliot is "All shall be well, and all manner of things shall be well." Notice that she does not gloss over the reality of sin and evil. Fourteenth-century Norwich was a place that knew war, plague, and famine. No, it is rather that she looks forward to a mysterious act of God that she does not attempt to explain, by which God's love will triumph over the very real sin and evil present in God's creation.

Because of her interest in the theological problems associated with evil in the world and her hope for a changed creation, Julian has one of the most balanced views when considered by the four dimensions of spirituality discussed in this book.

• DISCUSSION QUESTIONS

1. Have you experienced an Eastern Orthodox worship service? Tell about it.
2. What might Western Christians learn from Eastern sisters and brothers?
3. Which person in this chapter do you find most dramatic, appealing, or helpful in your own spiritual walk?
4. Compare and contrast the mysticism of Jan van Ruysbroeck and Julian of Norwich.

• EXERCISES: The Jesus Prayer and Icons

1. Quiet yourself as in the first exercise. Start by giving voice to the prayer by repeating "Lord Jesus, have mercy on me." You may wish to think the words silently, using the first phrase while inhaling and the second phrase while exhaling. To avoid hyperventilating, adapt the prayer to your normal breathing rather than trying to pace your breathing to the rate of the prayer. Although the words suggest contrition, the prayer may be used in any mood, whether of joy and thanksgiving or of sorrow and grief. Try praying this prayer for twenty minutes each morning and evening.

2. Icons provide a "right brain" approach to prayer. They give an image instead of words. Select an icon. First spend time centering yourself in silence, then put yourself in the presence of the icon. Regard it not as a simple picture but as a window through which you are steadily communing with another person. Put yourself on the other side of the window, and look at yourself lovingly, with all your faults and difficulties. Contemplate the other and yourself with compassion.

• AIDS FOR THE EXERCISES

Baggley, John. *Doors of Perception: Icons and Their Spiritual Significance.* Crestwood, N.Y.: St. Vladimir's Seminary Press, 1988.
Gillet, Lev. *The Jesus Prayer.* Crestwood, N.Y.: St. Vladimir's Seminary Press, 1987.
Nouwen, Henri J. M. *Behold the Beauty of the Lord: Praying with Icons.* Notre Dame, Ind.: Ave Maria, 1987.
Sjogren, Per Olof. *The Jesus Prayer.* London: SPCK, 1975.

• SUGGESTED READING

Jantzen, Grace M. *Julian of Norwich: Mystic and Theologian.* New York: Paulist, 1988.
Julian of Norwich. *Showings.* Classics of Western Spirituality Series. Translated by Edmund Colledge, O.S.A. and James Walsh, S.J. New York: Paulist, 1978.
Leclerq, Jean, O.S.B. *The Love of Learning and the Desire for God: A Study of Monastic Culture.* New York: New American Library, 1961.

Meyendorff, John. *Byzantine Theology: Historical Trends and Doctrinal Themes*. New
    York: Fordham University Press, 1987.
Ruusbroec, John. *John Ruusbroec: The Spiritual Espousals and Other Works*. Classics
    of Western Spirituality Series. Translated by James A. Wiseman, O.S.B. New
    York: Paulist, 1985. (This is simply another spelling for Jan van Ruysbroeck.)

5 | *Protestant and Catholic Reform*

The sixteenth century was a time of religious turmoil even greater than earlier centuries. Northern Europe broke away from the South and East in a wrenching struggle that was to divide Europe for more than four hundred years. Most thoughtful Roman Catholics agreed that reform was needed but held very different views. Those Catholics who became Protestant came to the view that not only did church political structures need reform, but so did theology, liturgy, sacraments, and spirituality. Separation from the papacy was the inevitable result.

Reformers who remained Catholic, on the other hand, managed to get approval at the Council of Trent for educational reform for priests, correction of obvious abuses by the bishops, and a more centralized administration of the church. The Catholics of Spain led the way in spiritual reform.

Both sides would transform Western Christendom, making a clear break from the later Middle Ages into the modern era.

The Protestant Reformation Reshaped Christian Spirituality

Luther and Lutherans Emphasized Grace and Freedom

A spiritual problem drove **Martin Luther** (1483-1546) to the extraordinary lengths of leading a Reformation. His search for a gracious God amid the many religious duties of late medieval piety could not satisfy him. Only when he understood Paul's words about the gospel and the righteousness of God in Romans 1 did the gates of paradise open. He understood for the first time that God's righteousness was a free gift, not a human achievement. He felt that he had been set free from the law of penances, pilgrimages, and monasteries, in order to love his neighbor in the ordinary deeds of daily life.

Unlike some other reformers, Luther did not want to abandon the Catholic heritage; he wanted to reform it. His norm was his understanding of the gospel, that people are justified by grace through faith. By this yardstick he decided to keep most of the mass, vestments, calendar, and architecture of the church.

But Luther introduced the vernacular Bible, hymn singing, and reform of Confession; he also oversaw the end of churchly pilgrimages (visiting distant holy places), relics (supposedly bones and artifacts related to biblical figures and saints), and vows of celibacy. These he saw as human attempts to merit what could never be merited but only received, the grace of God.

Just as we look back on the tradition today to decide what is helpful and what is not, so Luther did in his time. As he looked back on the writings of the Fathers and the mystics, he used the gospel articulated by Paul as the standard by which he judged the spiritual tradition. This led him to approve of some writers and disapprove of others.[1]

He loved to quote Augustine's anti-Pelagian writings and Bernard on the passive role of the soul before God. But he was not friendly to that stream of mysticism from Pseudo-Dionysius that became very philosophical in the hands of Meister Eckhart. Just as Luther came to see Aristotle as the great enemy in theology, so also in spirituality he opposed the foreign influence of Greek philosophy.

Luther's appreciation of the mystical tradition can be seen in his publication of the *Theologica Germanica*, an anonymous treatise from the previous century. Twice he saw this book through the press because he thought it helpful to the lay reader. His own more distinctive perspectives, however, came out in *The Freedom of a Christian* in 1520. In this treatise the mystical image of the marriage of the soul to Christ takes on a new significance: the exchange of Christ's righteousness for the soul's sin. It begins with paradoxical statements, a feature of Luther's thought on many subjects:

The Christian is a perfectly free lord of all, subject to none.
The Christian is a slave of all, subject to all.[2]

At the root of this paradox is Luther's view that the gospel has set us free from sin, death, and Satan, but the gospel also sets us free to serve our neighbors, as we become Christs to them.

Luther struggled with *Anfechtungen*, or spiritual attacks, all his life. *Anfechtung* meant deep despair, a challenge to his standing before God, falling into an abyss of guilt and the taunts of Satan. Luther did not view these experiences as inevitable parts of the spiritual journey, but as spiritual warfare with evil. The objective, sacramental side of his faith came to his rescue here, for he could answer, "I am baptized," and thus still his doubts, for he believed God had laid claim to him, however weak or sinful he might be.

In fact, Luther believed that Christians remain sinners all their lives. For all their good intentions and good works, all their prayers and Bible reading, they remained sinners, and their pious sins were sometimes worse than those of the flesh. He claimed that Christians are simultaneously saints and sinners; both condemned under the perfect law of God, and at the same time regarded by God as perfectly righteous because of the atonement of Jesus on the cross.

Thus he did not expect very much external change in Christian growth; he was suspicious of claims to growth in holiness and did not count such growth as his goal. Luther simply wanted to remain faithful to the cross as a sinner; no movement beyond that point seemed safe.

Luther's teaching on spirituality was very pragmatic, yet suspicious of methods to attain union with God. When asked by his barber how to pray, Luther replied with a very practical letter. In it he advises returning to the basics: the Ten Commandments, the Creed, and the Lord's Prayer. Make a garland, he advised, by finding in each part of these teachings something to learn, something for which to ask forgiveness, something to praise and thank God for, and a petition of aid for someone.[3]

This same return to the basics surely underlies Luther's *Small Catechism,* which has affected the spirituality of Lutherans ever since. In it Luther explains these same basic documents in a way parallel to Jesus' Sermon on the Mount, where he internalized the old commands of Israel, allowing no one to claim innocence.

Luther called for a "spirituality of the cross" as well as a "theology of the cross." The "theology of glory," which he opposed, stood outside the human condition to interpret everything as a great system, much as Aristotle had done and the medieval theologians were doing. Luther's "theology of the cross," however, began with the suffering of Christ on the cross which went against human reason and expectation. Here on the cross one finds God, Luther said. Here God is crucified and reveals his loving grace to humankind. A spirituality of the cross likewise is a following of Jesus through suffering and pain, not a triumphal vicarious thrill that elevates one to the heavens.

Luther's spirituality was focused on the freedom he experienced in finding a gracious God. It led to sharp criticism of parts of the Catholic spiritual tradition and new emphases on lay people, the Bible, and secular works as opposed to churchly acts of piety. His turbulent personality and earthy language were very different from our stereotypes of the calm, nice, heavenly minded "spiritual person."

Luther's strengths and weaknesses were partly inherited from Augustine. He focused almost exclusively on sin, forgiveness, and the cross, with little attention to healing, transformation, or resurrection. His low expectation for change in the Christian life has led to large numbers of "lukewarm" Lutherans. His view that love of self is the opposite of love for God or for neighbor has been very harmful. Yet his accent on grace and freedom are a matchless part of the Christian tradition.

In the century after Luther's death, his followers kept busy defending themselves and his teaching from Roman Catholics and from distortions within the Lutheran Church. This period, sometimes called the "Orthodox" or "Confessional" period, was a time of systematizing and defending Luther's teaching. Lutheran scholasticism came to base its theology on Aristotle just as

Catholic scholastics had done. Sermons came to be highly formal, academic denunciations of the errors of Catholics, Reformed, Anabaptists, and unorthodox Lutherans.

In this setting, a remarkable friendship developed between an older innovator and a young intellectual who became the prince of the Lutheran Orthodox theologians. **Johann Arndt** (1555-1621) was an innovator in the sense that his sermons and writings were not like those of his contemporaries. He was less interested in defending the "pure doctrine" of Lutheranism than in promoting genuine spiritual renewal in its followers.

His four books of *True Christianity* were a wake-up call to sleepy Lutherans, a prophetic call for awareness of sin, and a challenge to renewal through daily rebirth. He was accused of Catholic and heretical tendencies and was saved from condemnation only by his young friend Johann Gerhard (1582-1637), who had entered the ministry because of Arndt's influence on him at the age of fifteen. Gerhard himself was not deaf to the call for a Lutheran piety, as he wrote a small devotional book himself, but the spirit of the age had little time for the affections of the heart, preferring the polemical, the pedantic, and the rational.

Arndt laid the foundations for Lutheran Pietism, which would emerge in the late seventeenth century. He appreciated not only Luther's theology, but also his experience as a Christian. His contemporaries wanted to codify Luther; Arndt wanted people to discover Luther's experience of Christ. Clinging to Christ alone is the common theme of Luther and Arndt. Just as Luther was appalled by what he found in the parishes and returned to write the *Small Catechism*, so Arndt deplored the evils of his day and wrote *True Christianity*, which became the most influential book of devotion in the history of Lutheranism.

Jacob Boehme (1575-1624) did not fare as well. His writings were condemned as unorthodox, but he has continued to influence mystical writers and seekers down to the present day.

Luther was a dominating personality for his followers. Even today Lutherans revere and study him more than any other denomination does its founder. He never set out a system, but the vigor of his struggles and the forthrightness of his proclamation have marked not only those who still bear his name, but many others as well.

Yet the Lutheran tradition did not always follow Luther; it did not always even know him. Not until the twentieth century have his works been studied thoroughly. The tradition and the man stand in a dialogue, often in tension.

Reformed Protestantism Renewed the
Disciplines of Christian Life

The Reformed branch of Protestantism began in Switzerland under the leadership of **Ulrich Zwingli** (1484-1531), a contemporary of Luther. Zwingli went even further in his rejection of the Catholic tradition than did Luther, and the two clashed over the meaning and practice of the Lord's Supper at their only meeting, in 1529. Zwingli died shortly thereafter in battle against a Catholic army.

Zwingli wanted only a spirituality of the Word, with little or no emphasis on the liturgy or the sacraments. He put aside Catholic traditions such as the lectionary (Scripture readings appointed for certain days in the church year), vestments, musical instruments, and church visual art. To him these were distractions from the central matter: the Word. If the Bible did not command a given practice, that practice was surely an invention of the Papists and ought to be abandoned; it is said that he nailed shut his church organ.

Characteristic of Zwingli's spirituality is an emphasis on both inwardness and scriptural knowledge. He made a sharp distinction between inward and outward discipleship and regarded only the inward as valuable. Thus the outer was identified with "the world" and was seen as having little value.

What really counted was overcoming human ignorance by teaching the Bible. Thus the aesthetic, sacramental, and mystical dimensions of the Catholic tradition were put aside for the sake of a Bible-based rationalism that was to affect many parts of the Reformed tradition, including the Puritans of New England.

This part of the Reformed tradition is in tension with a more moderate strand coming from Calvin.

John Calvin (1509-64), a later reformer, barely escaped from France after the authorities learned of his Protestant views. He went out the back door while the police knocked on the front! Calvin wanted to be an "ivory tower" scholar, but the people of Geneva compelled him to settle there and direct the course of their experiment with a new religious and political order. There he inherited the Swiss tradition of Zwingli, who by this time was viewed as a martyr, so Calvin was not able to change it. For example, Calvin wanted weekly Communion services, as his piety was much more eucharistic, but Zwingli's four-times-a-year pattern had already taken hold.

The theology of Calvin is commonly known to include the teaching of predestination (the teaching of God's choice before creation of who should be saved), but the later Calvinism was often quite different from that of Calvin himself in its theological emphasis and its spirituality. Calvin's teaching grew out of a sense of God's sovereignty and love. If humans could not justify themselves, but only God could do so, then it followed logically that the gift of justification was God's to give to the ones who were chosen. The point of predestination for Calvin was the comfort of knowing that one's relationship to God was secure. One did not need to worry about the final judgment; God had already made the choice. Thus the believer could live in confidence, carrying out the will of God without anxiety.

The starting point for Calvin's spirituality was not predestination but the mystical union of the believer with Christ. He taught that humans are joined to Christ in baptism and that people grow in that union throughout life. Notice that this union is viewed quite differently from that of the mystics in the Catholic or Orthodox traditions. This mystical union is given to all Christians by faith, not as the end of a long road with progressive stages of growth. Thus every Christian is a "mystic," living in union with Christ, the way Paul speaks of being "in Christ" in the New Testament.

Calvin spoke of both justification and sanctification as divine gifts in this process. Fully agreeing with Luther that justification was by grace alone, he gave fuller emphasis to the simultaneous gift of sanctification, the theological term for the process by which people become holy.

Calvin places more emphasis on the spiritual disciplines, whereas Luther valued freedom from prescribed practices. Calvin's writing also shows his focus on the community, not just on the individual. He doubted the ability of the intellect to know the self, and he had a high regard for the power of language. Much more, he was awed by the power and sovereignty of God and of God's tenderness: he discussed God both as Father and as Mother of Christians.[4]

The Reformed tradition in Europe, like the Lutheran, went through a period of scholasticism, defining itself doctrinally. The spirituality of Zwingli often overshadowed that of Calvin, and the theology of Calvin was misinterpreted by placing predestination in the spotlight, rather than his ideas about mystical union. The Reformed tradition has kept alive better than some others, however, the concept of public responsibility for Christians. Reformed piety cannot remain indifferent to the sufferings of others in society; Christians have a responsibility for the health of the common life.

Anabaptists Called for Radical Discipleship in Small Fellowships

The various small groups who differed from both the Catholics and the Lutheran and Reformed churches were of great variety and were persecuted on all sides. Many of them affirmed "believers' baptism" and were thus called "re-baptizers" or Anabaptists, since most Europeans had already been baptized as infants. Their belief in baptism by immersion sometimes was cruelly parodied, as they were put to death by drowning.

These groups were feared and despised because their teachings not only differed radically from the Catholic-Protestant consensus, but had political, social, and economic implications that threatened the government. Some said that direct inspiration from God superseded the teaching of the Bible. They thus seemed to promote spiritual and political anarchy. The radical takeover of the city of Muenster in 1534-35 gave the movement a bad reputation in the eyes of both Catholics and Protestants. Two men took over as "kings," demanded total conformity to their views, approved of polygamy, and claimed that the kingdom of God had come to earth. Of course many Anabaptists did not approve of this "kingdom" either.

The common belief among such groups was that infant baptism was invalid; that just as in the New Testament accounts, one needed to choose to be baptized after coming to faith. Then one became a member of a select community, those persecuted by the world, being the only true disciples of Jesus, sharing the practice of the New Testament, including the rejection of public office or fighting in an army. There was great variety among these groups, some being pacifist, others militaristic.

Many of the radical sixteenth-century groups died out, but one that has remained to the present day is that of **Menno Simons** (1496?-1561). He gathered the fragments of various radical groups to form the fellowship we know as the Mennonites. Menno believed that a person in Christ is a new creature, and he assumed that those who were converted and baptized would no longer follow the ways of this world, but rather live without serious sin. The community of the church needed to be protected from false teaching and immoral actions by excommunicating those who trespassed. The Amish were the Mennonites who took this church discipline most seriously.

Thus Anabaptist spirituality has developed in the expectation of personal discipleship, separation from the fashions of the world, a strict moral code enforced by a close community, pacifism, simple life-style, and direct inspiration of the Holy Spirit.

Anglicans Found Unity in the
Book of Common Prayer

The Church of England experienced stormy reversals in the sixteenth century. The extremes of Roman Catholic and Reformed Protestant views produced famous martyrs and even civil war in the following century. It took a long time for the variety of viewpoints to be accommodated, but eventually the Anglican Church (Episcopalian in the United States) embraced wide differences in theological perspective. What has developed out of those experiences in our own day is a view of Anglicanism as a bridge among the Catholic, Protestant, and Orthodox traditions. Thus there is some question about classifying this church as Protestant since it sees itself as catholic in the sense of universal.

The Anglicans want to include as many views as possible within their communion and have agreed therefore not to be exclusive about theological or ethical views, but to be united in one form of worship: *The Book of Common Prayer*. They see worship as coming before theology as a basis for their unity. As one Anglican puts it, *"The Book of Common Prayer* is a rule of life. It is meant to describe, shape, and support the Anglican way of being Christian."[5]

The emphasis in Anglican spirituality is on the common liturgy as the context for personal growth. Thomas Cranmer was the first author of the prayer book (1549), but it has gone through many revisions since then. Praying the Psalms is a significant part of Anglican worship. The collects or common prayers of this collection reveal Anglican sensibilities and exquisite literary style.

The story of Anglican spirituality beyond the sixteenth century is one that includes many poets. Among the first were George Herbert (1593-1633), and John Donne (1571-1631), whose "metaphysical" poetry reveals startling images and deep devotion. Among the most influential of Anglican writers were Jeremy Taylor (1613-1667), who wrote *Holy Living* and *Holy Dying;* William Law (1686-1761), author of *A Serious Call to a Devout and Holy Life;* and John Keble (1792-1866), who composed *The Christian Year*.

Early Anglicanism contained the seeds for the three main branches of emphasis that developed more clearly later in its history. The liberal, or broad, church strand (eighteenth century) emphasized the role of the human intellect in appropriating and expressing the truth of God found in nature as well as in Scripture. The evangelical, or low church, strand (eighteenth century) emphasized the teachings of the Protestant reformers in Europe, with special emphasis on preaching for conversion and lively singing. The catholic, or high church, strand (nineteenth century) emphasized the role of bishops and sacraments, the early fathers of the church, and continuity with Roman Catholicism.

Anglicans have thus developed a strong tradition of spirituality with many strands. Communal worship stands at the center; personal piety is practiced in that context.

These four types of Protestant churches in the sixteenth century, the Lutherans, the Reformed, the Anabaptists, and the Anglicans, increased in number and variety as time passed. What all had in common was an emphasis on the Bible and a strong conviction of the need for reform of Roman Catholicism not only in various abuses, but also in basic principles and common practices of spirituality.

The Catholic Reformation

At the very time that some Catholics were leaving the church in frustration, others were working to curb the abuses that most people agreed were hindering its life. There was a great need for change in the institutional life of the church and for a response to the theological challenges of the Protestants.

The **Council of Trent** attempted to deal with both. It met sporadically in northern Italy from 1545 to 1563. The political side of the reforms were difficult. Progress was made, however, in improving education for priests and outlawing abuses by bishops. The office of bishop, for example, could no longer be sold to the highest bidder.

On the theological side, the council drew up doctrinal statements that defined Catholicism as distinct from Protestantism, defending what Protestants had attacked. The conservative, defensive response of Trent is understandable in its context, but is nevertheless regrettable: Catholics and Protestants rejected each other for four hundred years thereafter. Not until Vatican II in the 1960s was the door opened for serious conversation between these two branches of Christendom.

Ignatius of Loyola Founded the Jesuits, a New Type of Religious Order

About the same time that Luther was defending his teachings in Germany, **Ignatius of Loyola** (1491?-1556) experienced a profound conversion after reading spiritual literature. He was recuperating in a hospital after a serious wound in the Battle of Pamplona in 1521 when he read the life of Jesus and lives of the saints. He dedicated himself entirely to Jesus Christ and began writing one of the most powerful books in the history of Christian spirituality, his *Spiritual Exercises*.

After traveling to the Holy Land to fulfill a vow of thanksgiving, Ignatius took up theology in Paris. It was here that a group of like-minded persons gathered around him. This group eventually moved to Rome and received the pope's permission to form a new order, the Society of Jesus, in 1540. Ignatius was elected the superior general and spent the rest of his life leading the order from its headquarters in Rome.

The *Spiritual Exercises* are actually a manual written for a retreat director. The instructions are simultaneously very specific and very flexible. It was intended that the retreatant would spend thirty days, passing through four "weeks," during which a number of experiences would lead to discernment of the direction of life for that person. During the retreat the person would meet daily with a spiritual director, pray for four or five hours, participate in the mass, and keep silence. Ignatius himself, however, encouraged the director to adapt this program to individual needs, and the retreat is now often given in several shorter periods, except that Jesuits themselves still participate for the full thirty days.

The paradoxical feature of the *Exercises* is their appeal to the affections or emotions to accomplish their purpose, while remaining very rational. The retreatant's imagination is especially employed to reconstruct biblical scenes, in which the retreatants participate and feel the motions of their hearts. The program is designed to give individual freedom within a rather clear and fixed pathway, leading to a clear decision about how to follow Jesus. The daily examen (examination of conscience) is an important discipline described in the *Exercises*. It is an exercise in surrender to God and discernment of God's leading.

The Jesuit Order, which Ignatius founded, was to be a radical new form of monasticism. It went another step beyond the mendicant orders (Franciscans and Dominicans) to individualize the commitment to a religious order. Whereas "stability," the promise to stay in one place, was part of monastic vows, the Jesuits saw travel to wherever they were needed as their ascetic duty. Also the ideal of "contemplative in action" meant that the Jesuit did not always live in community, but was often alone, and for those who were together, there was no chanting of the Divine Office. This departure from the tradition meant that service to others was a higher priority than communal worship. Yet each Jesuit was expected to find time in the day to say his own office, that is, to pray the prayers and read the Scriptures appointed for that day.

Ignatius's ideals were formed partly by Paul, the same Paul who was the basis for Luther's reformation. But Ignatius and the Jesuits were totally opposed to Lutheranism, and they took special vows of loyalty and obedience to the pope. What inspired Ignatius was Paul's life-style as a missionary, his willingness to be all things to all people in order to save some.

Ignatius was also influenced by *The Imitation of Christ,* the only book other than the Bible that he recommended in the *Spiritual Exercises.* It is clear, however, that Ignatius had some significant differences from this book, notably in its denigration of academic and intellectual pursuits. His order was to become known for the highest standards of scholarship.

The Jesuits made use of three important practices, which they developed to a high degree of usefulness. The retreat, as defined in the *Spiritual Exercises,* was further defined in a *Directory* of 1599. Here the traditional three stages of spiritual life (purgative, illuminative, and unitive) were connected with the four weeks of the retreat.

Second, spiritual direction became a Jesuit specialty, growing out of the retreats. In later history, Jesuits came to be the confessors or directors for many of the powerful rulers of Europe and were suspected of using their influence directly for the pope.

Third, a number of sodalities or confraternities were formed in Jesuit schools. These were youth groups that met to encourage spiritual commitment among boys, some of whom would later become Jesuits themselves.

The ideal of travel for service, inspired by the apostle Paul, led many Jesuits to become missionaries to Latin America, Africa, and Asia, as well as to Europe. Two of the most notable were Matteo Ricci (1552-1610) in China and Roberto de Nobili (1577-1656) in India. They developed a high regard for their host cultures and went far (the pope said too far!) in adapting Christianity to those cultures. As a result, they gained adherents from some of the most powerful and well educated of those societies, but were not able to found lasting churches. This would prove to be a sharp contrast to much later mission history, where the poor and marginal members of society were attracted to Christianity by missionaries who did not much respect the host culture.

The early Jesuit balance between the mystical and the practical proved difficult to maintain after the death of Ignatius. The order veered toward a moralism and absolutism, a willingness to deceive and acquire secret information, which made it the fear of all Protestant rulers. Persons were accused of being Jesuits, and it was feared that they would try to overthrow Protestant rulers on behalf of Spain or France. Because of political activities the order was suppressed in 1774. It was reestablished in 1814 without the political intrigue and has become the largest single Catholic order in the world.

Teresa of Avila and John of the Cross
Renewed the Carmelite Order

Mother Teresa of Jesus (1515-82), as her contemporaries called her, is one of the great mystics and reformers of Spain. She had become a Carmelite, an order founded on Mount Carmel in the Holy Land in the mid twelfth century. Teresa became the leader of a reform movement that followed the early strict rule of the Carmelites rather than a more recent, mitigated one. The Reform movement came to be called "discalced," or shoeless. Teresa was involved in founding many new houses of nuns and in defending the Reform to many authorities.

It is as a mystic, however, that Teresa has had her greatest influence. Her *Life* gives a direct view of her trials and development. She describes her severe illness of 1538-39, her conversion to a deep spiritual life in 1554, and the vision of Christ sending a spear through her heart in 1559. The men around her did not know how to deal with her frequent visions and "locutions" (words from God), and told her that they must come from the devil. She was deeply troubled until she obtained sounder advice from another mystic.

The *Interior Castle* is a thoroughgoing analysis of spiritual development. In seven "mansions," she describes the soul's journey to God, from the purgative, through the illuminative, and to the unitive. She also classifies prayer, meditation, and contemplation. She writes of two kinds of passive contemplation, the prayer of quiet and the prayer of union, which were her daily practice.

Like her younger associate, John of the Cross, she indicates severe trials near the end of this journey. Her prose, however, is much more understandable than John's as she uses metaphors and experiences of daily life to explain her meaning. She also wrote poetry; but John is unequaled in verse.

The writings of **John of the Cross** (1542-91) reflect a life of dramatic reversals. John was invested with considerable responsibility by Teresa even as a young man, when he joined the Reform movement in the Carmelite Order. She had already founded the movement among the nuns; he was to found it among the monks. In fact, he became for a time the spiritual director of Teresa herself during the time she experienced what she called the "spiritual marriage."

John was later kidnapped and imprisoned in a dank cell for six months by his opponents in the order who were against the Reform movement. While in prison he began to compose poetry, first only mentally, and then on paper. After escaping from prison, he was elected again to responsible posts in the Reform branch of the Carmelites, and he wrote most of his prose works during the 1580s.

But because of his willingness to be a "whistle-blower," because of stating his frank opinion in a committee meeting with the vicar general of the order, he was stripped of all his offices and sent to an obscure post, where he became ill and died at the age of forty-nine.

Out of this life of passion and conflict, John wrote works on spiritual theology that led to his selection as a doctor of the Roman Catholic Church. His main works are *The Ascent of Mount Carmel, The Dark Night, The Spiritual Canticle,* and *The Living Flame of Love.* These prose works do not enjoy the same esteem as his poetry for stylistic excellence; his explanation of the poetry is often dense and repetitive. Nevertheless, his poetry is among the best ever written in the Spanish language. Here is a sample in translation:

> One dark night,
> Fired with love's urgent longings
> —Ah, the sheer grace!—
> I went out unseen,
> My house being now all stilled;
>
> In darkness, and secure,
> By the secret ladder, disguised,
> —Ah, the sheer grace!
> In darkness and concealment,
> My house being now all stilled; . . .
>
> O guiding night!
> O night more lovely than the dawn!
> O night that had united
> The Lover with His beloved,
> Transforming the beloved in her Lover.
>
> Upon my flowering breast
> Which I kept wholly for Him alone,
> There He lay sleeping,
> And I caressing Him
> There in a breeze from the fanning cedars.
>
> When the breeze blew from the turret
> Parting His hair,
> He wounded my neck

With his gentle hand,
Suspending all my senses.

I abandoned and forgot myself,
Laying my face on my Beloved;
All things ceased; I went out from myself,
Leaving my cares
Forgotten among the lilies.[6]

The most distinctive concept for which John is known is the dark night. He uses this metaphor in at least two ways: to describe the inability of the intellect to grasp God and to describe the experience of the soul on its journey to the mountaintop, to union with God.

In the first sense, John is saying something that had become widely accepted in the Middle Ages from the influence of Pseudo Dionysius: a negative theology that underlined the inadequacy of any concept or image to describe God. In the second, however, he was to give classic expression to the experience of lostness, confusion, drought, and panic that is often part of the spiritual path.

• DISCUSSION QUESTIONS

1. How would you compare the various strands of Protestantism in their various types of spirituality? Was the Protestant Reformation a revolution in spirituality, or was it simply a different mix of older elements?

2. Have you experienced something like a "dark night" of the soul? How was it like or unlike what John of the Cross describes?

3. What are the rewards and the difficulties in seeking to outline stages of spiritual growth as Teresa did?

4. Do differences in spirituality between Catholics and Protestants continue to this day? Have Catholics and Protestants moved closer than they were in the sixteenth century, with regard to spirituality?

• EXERCISES: The Lord's Prayer and the Examen

From Luther we learn of his simple method of prayer, and from Ignatius, the concept of the daily examen.

1. Spend some time in silence as discussed in chapter 1, exercise 1. Now take the Lord's Prayer one phrase at a time and "make a garland" for each one as Luther suggested. For each phrase, think of something to give thanks for, something to repent of, and some guidance for daily life. Then go on to the next phrase. If one thought is especially precious, stay with it. Do not worry about finishing the whole prayer.

2. The daily examen may be done in a variety of ways, but here is one that is helpful to me. At bedtime, briefly review the day, looking especially for grace notes from God and for problems that have arisen. Then the next morning examine the previous day in more detail. Use these words to guide your thinking: *insight, review,* *thanks, repentance,* and *renewal.* First, ask God the Holy Spirit for insight, for we do not really know ourselves very well. Seek to recognize what your own inclinations might pass over, whether gifts, strengths,.or sins. Then review the events of the day. Give thinks for all the gifts of the day. Repent and ask forgiveness for wrong choices or bad attitudes; ask for healing of neurotic guilt or broken relationships. Renewal means receiving God's forgiveness and strength for a new day as well as making very practical resolutions about what will help you in this day to avoid the pitfalls you have experienced before.

It is helpful to write down briefly some points each day that arise from the examen.

• AIDS FOR THE EXERCISES

Luther, Martin. "A Simple Way to Pray," *Luther's Works,* Vol 43. Philadelphia: Fortress, 1968. Pp. 187-212.
Trobisch, Walter. "Martin Luther's Quiet Time," *Complete Works of Walter Trobisch.* Downers Grove, Ill.: InterVarsity Press, 1987. Pp. 703-14.

• SUGGESTED READING

The Collected Works of St. John of the Cross. Translated by Kieran Kavanaugh and Otilio Rodriguez. Washington, D.C.: Institute of Carmelite Studies, 1979.
Ignatius, *Spiritual Exercises.* Classics of Western Spirituality Series. New York: Paulist, 1991.
Lull, Timothy F. *Martin Luther's Basic Theological Writings.* Minneapolis: Fortress, 1989.
Senn, Frank C., ed. *Protestant Spiritual Traditions.* New York: Paulist, 1986.
Teresa of Avila. *Interior Castle.* New York: Doubleday, 1989 (1961).

6 | The "Modern" Era

In the seventeenth to nineteenth centuries, Christianity faced many new challenges as it began to move from Europe to again become a transcontinental faith. After sputtering attempts by Portuguese and Spanish missionaries in the sixteenth century, Christianity came to the Americas by emigration, and then with a revived zeal, to Africa and Asia by a populist mission movement in the nineteenth century.

Much of Christian attention in this period, however, was focused on European and American problems such as new cultural developments, urbanization, the industrial revolution, and wars between nations. New approaches to spirituality were developed among the relatively young Protestant churches and in the Catholic and Orthodox churches as well.

The "Modern" Worldview Saw Itself as "Enlightenment"

The cultural changes in Europe from the fifteenth to the eighteenth centuries were so dramatic that people began to see themselves in an entirely new era. They looked back on history now in three main stages—the ancient, the middle (or medieval), and the modern. With the rise of a new style of learning, sometimes called humanism, in the fifteenth century, the theological method of scholasticism had been put in the shade. The rise of Protestantism ended the sole dominance of the Roman Catholic Church in European culture. The secular interests of the Renaissance placed the spiritual in a separate sphere.

The full implications of the Renaissance were not realized, however, until the 1700s, when a new movement, identified with rationalist thinkers such as Newton, Voltaire, Kant, Locke, and Franklin, emerged. It was later called the Enlightenment. The movement understood itself to be the dawn of a new day after the long night of the Middle Ages. Its implication was that the age of superstition was passing, and human beings now could use the clearheaded guide of their own reason to test every proposition claiming truth.

In the thirteenth century, Aquinas had welcomed reason as the divine gift to accompany and provide the basis for revelation. His synthesis of reason and revelation, nature and grace, was one of the great intellectual accomplishments of the Western church. His system was dismantled by the philosophers in such a way that revelation no longer had an independent claim to truth but had to be submitted to the judgment of what was thought reasonable. For example, miracles were not thought possible, but proving that a rational God existed was thought very reasonable. Yet *reason* is in fact a variable term; what is thought reasonable at one time may vary greatly from another. It was not long before the prevailing proofs of God's existence were challenged.

One contemporary theologian, Darrell Jodock, summarizes the "modern" with this list of themes: (1) autonomous reason, (2) progress and antitradition, (3) objectivity and an infatuation with science, (4) optimism, (5) individualism, and (6) mechanism. The modern worldview saw God as a distant, intelligent designer who set the universe going like a great clockwork and then left it to run on its own. Religion was largely reduced to morality, leaving little room for an affective spirituality.

In the late twentieth century many people believe that we are again moving into a new era and that the modern paradigms of science and philosophy no longer fit our experience. Thus many writers speak of the post-modern era, not yet giving a name to the new age, but indicating that the assumptions that framed the seventeenth to the nineteenth centuries are becoming obsolete. New paradigms demand new theologies and new spiritual styles.

Yet much of our European and North American way of thinking in the twentieth century is still orientated to those assumptions. We are still secularists, separating spirituality from the "real world"; we still think of science as the arbiter of that real world; we are still optimistic about technological progress; and we are still individualists.

It is the period of the Enlightenment, I am convinced, that separates the Western world from the rest of the world. The assumptions and the continuing effects of the Enlightenment make a gap between Christians in Europe and North America and their brothers and sisters elsewhere. It is important to see how this period has affected Christian spirituality for good or ill.

Protestants Regained Spiritualities
of the Heart

After the period of reformation, many of the Protestant movements went through three periods of development. The first was a confessional period, when the attention of the leaders was focused on defining and defending the denomination intellectually. The second was a Pietist period, calling for more attention to the needs of ordinary people, especially in the affective dimension of the spiritual life. And finally, the rationalist period, or Enlightenment, described above, brought the critique of an autonomous reason to bear on both the Bible and the practices of the churches. Rationalism reduced the role of religion to teaching universal ethical norms and so had little emphasis on personal relations to God or the death and resurrection of Jesus.

It should be noted that in the English-speaking world, the periods of Pietism and rationalism overlapped; each was competing with, and to some degree influencing, the other. For example, John Wesley read John Locke and was very much interested in empirical verification. Across the Atlantic, Benjamin Franklin went to hear the evangelist George Whitefield and could not prevent himself from contributing all his coins to Whitefield's orphanage project.

Puritans, Quakers, Pietists

The **Puritan** movement in the Church of England began as early as the 1500s but continued into the 1700s to Jonathan Edwards, "the last Puritan." The purpose of the movement was to purify the Anglican church along Reformed Protestant lines. Thus it took its inspiration from the teachings of Zwingli in Zurich and Calvin in Geneva. The popular view of Puritans is thought to be unfair by many scholars who have studied the movement. The Puritans were more affirming of human work, play, and sexuality than they are given credit for.

The central idea of Puritan spirituality was personal faith, conviction, and self-scrutiny. Nothing could be accepted that was imposed from the outside. Hypocrisy was abhored; individual experience and conviction valued.

The Sabbath day became the mainspring of the Puritan calendar, as the annual calendar of the Roman Catholic Church with Advent and Lent was discarded. The Sabbath day was to be devoted to religious pursuits, with emphasis on hearing the Word preached and on receiving the sacrament of the Lord's Supper.

Puritans did experience raptures comparable to those of the Roman Catholic mystics, though they would abhor the comparison. They were also free to use erotic metaphors for these intense experiences and frequently quoted the Song of Songs or Bernard's spiritualized version, in which the lovers are Christ and the soul.

Puritan theology was meant to lead to an assurance that one was indeed predestined (chosen) by God for salvation. Like many other forms of Christian spirituality, the Puritans thought that their life in God was so important that halfway measures were not possible: Christianity demanded the whole of personal and social life.

John Bunyan (1628-88) wrote one of the most influential English Christian classics, *Pilgrim's Progress*, from prison. As a Puritan he shared the fate of many of his companions. The book is an allegory of the Christian life, using a protagonist named Christian who on his way to the Celestial City meets such trials and temptations as Vanity Fair, the Slough of Despond, and the Delectable Mountains. The basic metaphor of life as a journey is a rich one. It is clear from this story that Bunyan and other Puritans did not see Christian spirituality as a hobby for "couch potatoes," but as a vigorously challenging struggle with the world and one's own desires. His allegory inflamed the spirituality of Protestants for centuries to come.

Contemporaries of the Puritans, and often in conflict with them, were the Quakers, the group that called itself the **Society of Friends,** and continues its witness for peace up to the present day. There are parallels here to the radical wing of the Reformation in Germany: in both places the new sects were persecuted and feared for undermining religious teaching and threatening the foundations of public order (see chapter 5).

George Fox (1624-91), the founder of the Quakers, believed that the Holy Spirit spoke directly through people, to what he called "that of God in every man." This inspiration seemed to rank higher than the Scripture and so was opposed by the churches. The charismatic early meetings for worship, without clergy or sacrament, depended on individuals to wait in silence for the inspiration of the Spirit, and to hear what others were led to say.

Quakers in America were distinguished from other Christians by their witness for peace and fair dealing with all peoples. William Penn, founder of Pennsylvania, is reputed to have dealt more fairly with American Indians than other early colonists did. His Quaker convictions led to a respect for native people not shown by others.

Later the Quakers were the first Christian denomination to publicly oppose slavery. They were tugged in this direction by the tender conscience of **John Woolman** (1720-72). He came to abhor slavery and spent much of his life personally confronting slave owners and speaking in Quaker meetings. His *Journal* is a book of inspiration still widely read.

The Quakers demonstrate a spirituality that is simple and wholistic: social justice actions are not separate from listening to the Spirit. Though we may smile at their refusal to take off their hats or address officials as "you" instead of "thee," the same principles that led to these offensive actions led the Quakers to oppose war and stand for the rights of Indians and African slaves. Their spirituality led them to oppose social convention on all levels, and many early Quakers suffered prison and death for their courageous discipleship.

In Germany Lutheran **Pietism** was a movement of church reform begun by **Philip Jacob Spener** (1635-1705) under the influence of Arndt (see p. 72). Like Arndt, he saw the church as passive and indifferent, not aware of the true Christianity of the Gospels. Like Arndt, he called for self-examination, repentance, and conversion. Like Arndt, he tired quickly of the polemics that seemed to dominate Lutheran sermons.

What Spener did that went beyond Arndt was to publish a program of church reform and to organize groups to accomplish it. The book was *Pia Desideria* ("pious hopes"), which unlike its title was very concrete in its proposals. Most of these would not sound radical today. He called for midweek Bible studies, lay activism in the church, sermons that built up the hearer instead of arguing with other preachers or showing off classical learning, and seminaries that taught pastoral care. In his day these were seen as radical, and he faced considerable ostracism, leading even to forced departure from his parish in Frankfurt.

The social side of Pietist reform was developed by **August Herman Francke** (1663-1727), who was not only a professor of theology at Halle, but the founder of institutions for social help. He started orphanages, schools, and a library. Francke also trained some of the first Protestant missionaries to leave Europe. B. Ziegenbalg (1682-1719) and H. Plütschau traveled to India under Danish sponsorship. They made a good start in studying Indian religion and culture, as well as publishing books for India.

Later, Pietism spread to Scandinavian Europe. In Norway, Hans Nielsen Hauge (1771-1824), a traveling lay preacher, was imprisoned for over seven years for leading unauthorized spiritual meetings. In Sweden, Carl Olof Rosenius (1816-68) preached widely, edited *The Pietist* magazine, founded a mission society, and composed many popular hymns.

Thus the pietist movement emphasized personal conversion, with the expectation of a renewed life, an outer change coming from inner rebirth. It broke new ground in Bible study for the laity, social institutions, and foreign missions. The Pietists insisted that Christianity is a life to be lived and not just a mental faith. Yet the remarks of Tertullian on spectacles would have been approved by strict Pietists. The dark side of the movement was a growing anti-intellectualism, a tendency to feel self-righteous, and a legalism that made all pleasure something "worldly." The film "Babette's Feast" affectionately shows Danish Pietists overcoming their opposition to the pleasures of taste at a sumptuous banquet prepared by a French Roman Catholic.

Evangelicals and Methodists

Similar to the Pietists were the **evangelicals**, who emerged in the following century in England and New England. The 1700s were an age in which both rationalism (witness the U.S. Constitution) and evangelicalism (witness the rise of the Methodists) developed. Evangelicalism seems an obvious foil to rationalism, and yet it shared many of rationalism's assumptions. It had an inquiring practical bent; Wesley was willing, one might say, to do scientific research in the realm of the spiritual by waiting to see which religious experiences were valid and which led nowhere.

We can describe early evangelicals in three settings: the Anglican Church, the Methodist movement, and the Congregationalist churches of New England. What all had in common was preaching for repentance, expectation of a changed life after conversion, and room for expressions of emotion not always tolerated in the previous denominations.

The Anglican branch of this movement was not led by any single person. Perhaps one of the best known in North America is **John Newton** (1725-1807), because he was the author of the beloved hymn "Amazing Grace." Newton had been a captain in the slave trade, was dramatically converted, and became an Anglican priest, dying in the pulpit. Like other evangelicals, he believed in early rising for prayer, Bible reading as an indispensable part of devotion, and the gathering of the family for group prayers.

In its second generation, Anglican evangelicalism produced one of the outstanding social reformers of the modern era, **William Wilberforce** (1759-1833), whose persistent voice in the British Parliament led to the abolition of the trans-Atlantic slave trade in the early 1800s. His prayer life is said to have given him the perseverance over the decades necessary for the passage of this legislation. A leading member of the Clapham Sect, a fellowship of wealthy evangelicals, he wrote *A Practical View of the Prevailing System of Professed Christians in the Higher and Middle Classes in This Country Contrasted with Real Christianity.*

In the third generation came **Henry Venn** (1799-1873), the general secretary of the Church Mission Society, who advocated "self-governing, self-supporting, and self-propagating churches" instead of continued missionary dependency in Africa and Asia. His concept is fundamental to the practice of indigenous Christian spirituality. Ahead of his time, Venn advanced Samuel Ajayi Crowther to be the first African bishop in the Anglican Church. When Crowther died in 1891 (long after Venn), he was replaced by a European bishop. This led to the founding of some of the first African indigenous churches, whose spirituality was to be much more African.

The Methodist story of the 1700s is full of drama and opposition. **John Wesley** (1703-91) and his brother Charles became uncommonly devoted Christians, partly through the reading of the *Imitation of Christ* and British devotional writers. With a few other students the Wesleys formed a group for regular prayer, Holy Communion, and prison visitation at Oxford University. The group came to be ridiculed with names such as "The Holy Club" and "Methodists." Their daily time schedules and other strict requirements led to this charge of "Method-ism." But it was to be years before the Methodists emerged as a Christian denomination.

John and Charles, on their way to be missionaries in Georgia, encountered the Moravians, a group similar to Lutheran Pietists. John made a mess of his work in America, insisting on strict rules and refusing Communion to a woman who left him for another man. He had to leave under threat of arrest. Furthermore, all his righteous striving had not given him peace with God. On his return to England he continued his contact with the Moravians, and at one of their meetings on Aldersgate Street, he was able to come to personal faith in Christ and peace of heart. He described this experience in a famous passage in his *Journal* for May 24, 1738. Someone was reading from Luther's preface to the Epistle to the Romans.

> About a quarter before nine, while he was describing the change which God works in the heart through faith in Christ, I felt my heart strangely warmed. I felt I did trust in Christ, Christ alone for salvation; and an assurance was given me that he had taken away *my* sins, even *mine*, and saved *me* from the law of sin and death.[1]

Ever after this, Wesleyan spirituality has been known as the spirituality of the warm heart. His new emphases gradually made him unwelcome in Anglican churches. These rejections led John Wesley to begin preaching outside church buildings in fields and in the streets. His parish, he said, was the world, and he traveled constantly, often preaching five times a day. He said he wanted to spread Scriptural holiness over the land. In other words, he looked for practical changes in the lives of the converted.

One of those changes was avoiding gin, which had been the ruin of many families. Instead of spending money on gin, he encouraged saving money in "thrift clubs," and he wrote pamphlets on improving one's health. These habits took hold among many poor Methodists to such a degree that English society was changed, and the Methodists tended to move out of poverty.

The most contentious teaching of Wesley concerned Christian perfection. Wesley understood the biblical passages on perfection (e.g., Matt. 5:48; 1 John 3:4-10) to mean that the work of sanctification could follow justification and lead to perfect love in the intentions of the believer. Furthermore, he taught that some persons experienced this "entire sanctification" as a "second blessing," an instantaneous experience. Wesley never claimed this for himself but reported it of several of his followers.

The spirituality of John Wesley himself was different from that of his followers. He was educated and committed to the Anglican Church. He liked to read the New Testament in Greek and critically read the Eastern Orthodox and Catholic mystics. Frequent Communion was important to him.

But many of the early Methodists were not highly educated and had little interest in the history of spirituality. Their practical experience was that the Anglican Church, comfortable in its upper-class culture, was not especially friendly to them. Reading the Word was more important than attending Communion services. So after his death, the Methodists went against the wishes of John Wesley and formed a separate denomination.

Charles Wesley (1707-88) did not travel as John did. He stayed at home, raised a family, and wrote five thousand hymns. He was surely one of the greatest of English hymn writers, bringing together biblical language, emotional power, and poetic beauty. A spirituality can be expressed in hymns, and Charles' collections surely had much to do with shaping not only Methodist piety, but also Protestant devotion throughout the English speaking world.

Evangelical faith, whether of Luther or of the Wesleys, longs to sing the praise of its Savior.

Oh, for a thousand tongues to sing my great Redeemer's praise,
The glories of my God and King, the triumphs of his grace![2]

The Wesleyan heritage was to produce many branches, not only the large Methodist churches in the United States, but also the smaller holiness groups founded in the 1800s, such as the Salvation Army and the Church of the Nazarene. The former concentrated on urban evangelism among the poor, the latter on developing the doctrine of complete sanctification.

French Roman Catholics Enhanced Spiritual Direction

There were a number of French Catholic spiritual writers in the modern period whose influence has gone beyond France and beyond the Roman Catholic Church. The first of these was **Francis de Sales** (1567-1622), whose *Introduction to the Devout Life* is still in print.

As Catholic bishop of Geneva, Switzerland, de Sales was very much involved both in preaching Catholic Reformation tenets from the Council of Trent and in giving spiritual direction to individuals. He came to write the *Introduction* as a means of reaching many others, and his clear style and use of many illustrations showed his intent that "devotion," or holiness, was for everyone, not just for the clergy or religious. He corresponded with Jane de Chantal and others who became spiritual directors in their own right.

De Sales's teaching is positive in tone—one might say optimistic—but his underlying intent is very serious. He made a clear distinction between the will and the emotions. For him the commitment of the will to God was to be resolute, whatever the emotional distractions.

Cardinal Pierre de Berulle (1575-1629), called the founder of the French school of spirituality, was influenced by personal contact with de Sales and by reading the church fathers, Ruysbroeck, and Saint Teresa of Avila. He helped to introduce Saint Teresa's Discalced Carmelites (see p. 79) into France. The most important feature of his spirituality is Christocentrism, that is, its focus on Jesus Christ. The Incarnation and the eucharistic presence of Christ are central. Unlike de Sales, however, Berulle and the French school tend to be pessimistic about human nature and severe in ascetic practice.

Nicholas Harmon, better known as **Lawrence of the Resurrection** (1611-91), was a lay brother in the Discalced Carmelites. His work in the kitchen did not draw much attention until the time of his death, when his superior interviewed him concerning his spirituality. Those interviews together with letters found after his death constitute the little devotional classic, *The Practice of the Presence of God*. Brother Lawrence describes how he focused on God not simply at quiet hours of prayer, but in the midst of his daily work: washing pots and pans.

> My most ordinary state is this simple attention, and this general, loving gaze upon God, to which I often find myself attached by sweetness and satisfaction greater than that which a baby feels at the breast of his nurse. If I dared to use the expression, I would willingly call this state "the breast of God," because of the inexpressible sweetness that I taste and experience in it.[3]

One of the greatest influences of the French school on popular piety was devotion to the Sacred Hearts of Jesus and Mary. The theme of the heart was a reference to the love of Jesus and of Mary toward the faithful, by the passion of the cross. The movement emphasized the humanity of these exalted figures. The roots of this devotional movement can be found in de Sales and Berulle, but the populizers were Saint John Eudes and Marguerite-Marie Alacocque. Her visions influenced the Jesuits to adopt the new devotion, which seemed too emotional to many church leaders.

Later developments in France led to the denunciation of both **Quietism** and **Jansenism** by the Roman Catholic Church. The complexities of these movements make it impossible to describe them within the limits of our space. The roots of Quietism go back at least to Miguel de Molinos (b. 1628), who, for reasons that are not clear, was condemned by Pope Innocent XI. Molinos seems to have taught such an abandonment to God that all things become indifferent to the soul, including the soul's own salvation, and thus, ultimately the soul's relation to God. Therefore the love of God paradoxically produces indifference to God. This is the view condemned as Quietism.

Accused of a similar teaching were Mme. **Jeanne-Marie Bouvier de la Mothe Guyon** (1648-1717) and her advisor **François Fenelon** (1651-1715), archbishop of Cambrai, in France. Fenelon came to be accepted into the highest circles of French society and was in charge of the education of King Louis XIV's grandsons. He introduced Guyon to these circles, and when her writings were condemned, he refused to join in attacks on her character and thus was exiled from the court. Guyon spent four years in the Bastille, and Fenelon was forced into obscurity.[4] He wrote a courageous letter to Louis XIV, frankly denouncing his war policies that brought suffering to many for the sake of the king's personal glory.

Fenelon was involved in spiritual direction by letter, like his admired predecessor, Francis de Sales. Because this advice was not lost in oral speech, but was preserved in writing, his advice still speaks to twentieth-century Christians. He is especially helpful for those of us who are continually too hard on ourselves.

> "Just as water quenches fire so do scruples act on prayer": whenever I think of you, Madame, those words come into my mind. . . . Every time you insist, against your better judgment, on undertaking these self-examinations which

have been so often condemned you disturb and upset yourself, dry yourself up, make prayer impossible and so remove yourself from God. . . . You are also taken up almost exclusively with yourself. Tell me, can all this be the work of God? . . . You should employ that delicate scrupulosity of yours against your own scruples and ask yourself if it can be right under pretext of discovering minute faults of behaviour to cause the well-springs of grace emanating from prayer to dry up, and to commit crass errors in order to subtilize little ones.[5]

Fenelon had a great deal to say about abandonment to God, which he describes this way: "True abandonment simply means letting oneself fall into the arms of God as a child falls into the arms of its [sic] mother."[6]

Jeanne Guyon was theologically uneducated but very sensitive spiritually. She has been decried as "hysterical" by many writers then and since, but there may be implicit sexism in these judgments. Her willingness to express all of her feelings in her writings, sometimes in excessive ways, weakened her defense; she and Fenelon were declared guilty of Quietism.

Those condemned as Quietists focused on the abandonment to God's providence, the passive reception of God's grace. The Jansenists, on the other hand, who were involved in the condemnation of the Quietists, rather concentrated on the active working out of one's salvation. The moral purpose in Christian living was emphasized in spite of a renewed teaching of Augustine's doctrine of predestination. Predestination ultimately led to the condemnation of the Jansenists also. The Jesuits, strong defenders of free will since Reformation times, were vigorous opponents of Jansenism.

It was from a Jansenist background that a distinctive French writer, Blaise Pascal, emerged.

Pascal and Kierkegaard Developed a
New View of Selfhood

Two writers who seem to stand apart from their traditions and do not easily fit any of the groups we have spoken about are Blaise Pascal and Søren Kierkegaard. **Blaise Pascal** (1623-62), who lived in France, was a brilliant scientist and mathematician. Both writers have been seen as influential founders of the existentialist movement in the twentieth century, but neither shares the views of twentieth-century existentialists.

Like Kierkegaard, Pascal exercised outstanding literary ability; his *Provincial Letters* are still studied as models of French style. He gathered fragments of ideas for a rational defense of the Christian faith, which was published after his death as *Pensees* ("thoughts"). In these writings his stance was that of the individual awed by the wonders of the universe, trying to decide whether to trust the Christian message or not. He wrote of the wager that every human being must make, betting one's life on the truth of the faith. He argued that it was better to live as a Christian and be disappointed after death than to live as an atheist and be wrong in the end.

Pascal is well known for his line, "The heart has its reasons of which reason knows nothing" (*Pensees*, 423). By saying this he was rejecting the narrowing of evidence for the Creator and Redeemer. Pascal was a layperson not trained in theology, and he did not have wide influence in his own day, but his remarks have been treasured not only in France but throughout the Christian world.

A lonely Danish Protestant voice of the nineteenth century takes a similar but distinctive stance on Christian spirituality. **Søren Kierkegaard** (1813-55) was a loner from his youth. After studying theology and philosophy, he came to reject both the reigning philosophy, that of Hegel, and the dominant form of Christianity, the Lutheran folk church. He could not identify with the intellectuals or with the Pietists. Sensing a divine call to devote himself totally to writing, he broke his engagement with Regina Olson. After that, he wrote some forty books in only fifteen years, which he later called his "authorship." On the one hand, the books attacked the reigning orthodoxies and set out his own new philosophy; on the other, they developed "edifying discourses" for the individual believer.

Kierkegaard's former set of books was written pseudonymously, under a variety of names, with marvelous literary and philosophical skill. In those books he sets forth not only a new way of thinking about historical and philosophical problems, but also his doctrine of the three stages of life. He does not write *about* the stages, but from *within* them. That is, he assumes the standpoint of each stage by creating fictional authors and demonstrates what the world looks like from that point of view.

Kirkegaard exemplifies (1) the aesthetic stage in volume 1 of *Either/Or*, a collection of writings including "The Diary of a Seducer." This stage views life in terms of pain and pleasure only. Then in volume 2 he demonstrates (2) the moral stage through the writings of a judge about his marriage. Here the categories become right and wrong. And finally he writes of (3) a religious stage, which takes the holy as the primary category but includes the aesthetic and moral within it. The religious stage, which Kierkegaard points to as necessary, is that of the "knight of faith," the individual who breaks out from the stifling crowd to follow God whatever the cost.

This is a radically different proposal from the traditional three stages of the mystical life. It is a change in consciousness demonstrated by characters. There is no explicit discussion of union with God, but rather trusting God without evidence, which Kierkegaard compares to floating over fifty thousand fathoms of water.

The second type of book in Kierkegard's "authorship" is devoted to edifying discourses. These books call on Kierkegaard's beloved reader, the individual, to ponder short passages of Scripture. Significant metaphors appear in these writings, such as the rich prince who loves a poor woman and wants to court her but cannot do so from his magnificent carriage. He must become poor to woo her. This becomes a model of the incarnation. One of Kierkegard's famous titles that has become an epigram in our day is *Purity of Heart Is to Will One Thing*.

Kierkegaard calls upon his reader to become a real self. He sees selfhood not as a given, not to be taken for granted. Rather "I" must become a self through the choices I make.

Kirkegaard was a harsh critic of the Lutheran Church of his day and was not liked by his contemporaries. Although he was Lutheran in his understanding of justification, he scathingly charged that Lutheran free grace was being misappropriated, taken for granted, in a system where everyone assumed themselves to be Christian. Thus one's Christianity became an easy, unimportant matter. On the contrary, Kierkegaard amazed everyone by saying that he was *not* a Christian, that this title was too high for him to claim. He hoped to make people stop and think about the commitment entailed in being a Christian.

Kierkegaard was an intellectual, and many of his philosophical works are difficult to understand. But his edifying discourses are written simply and directly. They are difficult, not because of terminology, but because of their demands on the will and the affections.

What is missing in Kierkegaard is a sense of the communal character of Christian faith. Because of his own life experience, he drew a picture of Christian spirituality that was individualist in the extreme. Further, the issues that engaged him did not include the relationship to nonhuman creation. Thus he is mostly focused on relationships to God and self.

One of the many valuable features of Kierkegaard, however, is his ability to skewer facades of spirituality. It is a special danger for people who *study* spirituality to think they are *living* it. His disdain for preachers dressed in fine robes, preaching about the crucifixion to make money, also applies to the aesthete who dabbles in spirituality as a sort of interesting hobby.

Orthodoxy Produced the *Philokalia*
and *The Way of a Pilgrim*

Eastern Orthodox spirituality has a way of drawing upon its Holy Tradition, which renews it age after age. Under the rule of Muslim Turks, long after the death of the Byzantine Empire, the Greek church renewed itself by reading the collection assembled by **Nicodemus of the Holy Mountain** (1749-1809) and **Macarius of Corinth** (1731-1805). This collection, entitled *Philokalia* ("the love of beauty"), drew upon writers in Eastern Christendom from the fourth to the fifteenth centuries. Among its themes were the Jesus Prayer, the need for personal spiritual direction, and the virtues needed not only by monks but laity who seek to know union with God. The book, first published in 1782, was soon translated into Slavonic and Russian, but only recently into

English. It has become perhaps the most influential book in Orthodox spirituality up to the present day. Its teachings follow Evagrius but surprisingly do not include any writings by the Cappadocians or Pseudo-Dionysius.

This multivolume set was expensive and not readily accessible. Most people in Russia were not able to afford it. But one anonymous writer popularized its message in a much shorter work, *The Way of a Pilgrim*. It appeared in 1884 and has remained the popular approach to the Jesus Prayer ever since.

The book tells of the longing of a Russian pilgrim to know the meaning of the constant prayer Paul urges in 1 Thessalonians 5:17, "Pray without ceasing." Since the book is a narrative, the reader's interest is focused on what will happen next, as the pilgrim seeks help for over a year and finally finds what he seeks with an old man who says:

> But what is prayer? And how does one learn to pray? Upon these questions, primary and essential as they are, one very rarely gets any precise enlightenment from present-day preachers. . . . The continuous interior prayer of Jesus is a constant uninterrupted calling upon the divine Name of Jesus with the lips, in the spirit, in the heart, while forming a mental picture of His constant presence, and imploring His grace, during every occupation, at all times, in all places, even during sleep. The appeal is couched in these terms, "Lord Jesus Christ, have mercy on me." One who accustoms himself to this appeal experiences as a result so deep a consolation and so great a need to offer the prayer always, that he can no longer live without it, and it will continue to voice itself within him of its own accord. Now do you understand what prayer without ceasing is?[7]

The pilgrim's adventures while praying constantly are more interesting than other writers' long theological discussions of the meaning of the prayer. The book has now been translated into many languages, and is available in English.

Mission Spirituality Motivated
Cross-Cultural Ministry

The earlier Catholic missions of the sixteenth and seventeenth centuries had not planted lasting churches for a number of reasons. In spite of a few notable exceptions among the Jesuits, the mission stations were often staffed by unworthy personnel who had no training or preparation for the work and little or no support from their orders. Further, the mission work was an ancillary arm of nationalist imperialism, so that control by Spain or Portugal, or gaining wealth by gold or slaves, was higher in priority than proclaiming the Savior. Thus most of the sixteenth-century churches in Africa and the Americas died out.

A few outstanding missionaries, such as Bartholomew de las Casas, spoke out against the abuses of soldiers and traders. His writings remain today as the most severe indictment of the Spanish treatment of American Indians.

Others such as Jean de Breboef suffered on the nomadic trails of the Great Lakes, patiently learning the Huron language, only to be captured by the Hurons' enemies and tortured to death.

The unshakable conviction of those early Catholic missionaries and the continuing basis for the missions from Europe and North America that came later was the conviction that salvation was only possible for the world's people if they heard the word of the cross, believed its message, and were baptized and became part of the church. This led most of them to overlook the damage that was done to native cultures by Europeans.

Both missionaries and the peoples among whom they served assumed that religion and culture were fixed together in such a way that becoming European was essential to becoming Christian. This assumption is like that of early Jewish Christians who demanded that Gentile converts become Jews before they could be Christian. Paul passionately disagreed. So do I. This book asserts that it is possible to be authentically Christian in any culture. There will indeed be tension between Christianity and any culture (if the Christian message is not watered down and domesticated too much by economic or political interests), but there will also be gifts that every culture can bring to the understanding of Christianity, just as Christianity has the gift of the good news of God's love for every culture.

Eastern Orthodox missionaries had earlier spread the faith from the Mediterranean into the Slavic lands. Their new outreach was to the east in Siberia and by the 1700s to Alaska.

Protestants did not get involved in overseas missions until more than a century after the Reformation. Finally, with the emergence of Pietism, the continental Moravians and Lutherans began sending missionaries in the 1700s. In Great Britain William Carey (1761-1834) began the effort. As a young Baptist shoemaker, he came to the conviction that God wanted him to travel to India with the message of Christ. His elders assured him that it could not be done and that if God wanted it done, "he surely would not choose *you, young man!*" But Carey pressed on, actually traveling to India himself.

Why did the missionaries go, often at great discomfort and danger to themselves? Of course there were unworthy reasons, as all human decisions are ambiguous. But on the positive side, missionary spirituality included love for the people served; courage in facing the unknown; confidence in God's provision when human help often failed; and ultimately a sense of humor over the tangled human condition, with all its different customs and languages.

For Catholics it was mainly members of religious orders who traveled. Until the late nineteenth century the vast majority were men. They belonged to some of the orders we have already spoken about, the Jesuits, the Franciscans, and the Dominicans. But new orders were founded in the nineteenth century, specifically for mission work. The Society for Mission to Africa, or "White Fathers," is an example.

On the Protestant side, mission societies took up the work before denominations did. The Church Mission Society of the Anglicans was one of the first, in 1799. The first American society was founded in 1814. American women became especially active in the late 1800s, founding their own societies and sending single women as well as married ones to serve all over the world. Women gave sacrificially for the support of their missionaries. The women missionaries themselves were often able to fulfill responsible posts that were denied to them at home. Eventually these societies were induced to unite with general societies, and the special role of women was gradually lost.

Missionary spirituality includes the spirituality of the missionaries themselves, but also that of their supporters at home. A certain global perspective is one aspect of such a spirituality. Another is fervent prayer, especially intercessory prayer. Mission supporters are called to a spirituality of love for people whom they have never seen.

The analogue to missionary spirituality is that of the peoples who were first won to Christianity through their efforts. The very first generation of Christians were highly committed to the faith, and some were prepared to give their lives when persecuted. Among these were the Ugandan martyrs killed in 1885-86. The era of Christian martyrs did not end in 313, but continues up to the present day.

It is in the twentieth century that most of the indigenous Christian movements in different continents have developed a distinctive voice. To that century we turn next.

• **DISCUSSION QUESTIONS**

1. Do you see signs of a conflict between the modern, or Enlightenment, view of things, and a postmodern viewpoint?

2. What is the stereotype of a Puritan? What more can be said about Puritans?

3. What was distinctive about the views of Pascal and Kierkegaard compared to what came before them?

4. Is mission an integral part of Christian spirituality or an aberration? What are proper ways of proclaiming the good news of Jesus, and what are improper ways?

• **EXERCISES: Journaling and Spiritual Direction**

1. Seventeenth- and eighteenth-century Christians were faithful in journaling. They recorded not only the outer events of their lives, but also their inner thoughts and feelings.

Putting things on paper is one way to get them out where they can be dealt with. Journaling is a good partner to the daily examen. Look for the signs of God's love in your daily life, and write them down. Read over your journal periodically to sense the path you have trod, and to seek guidance for the path ahead.

It is especially helpful to write out prayers. Experiment by writing the longings of your heart in a prayer to God. It takes longer than speaking, of course, but gives you time to ponder.

2. A spiritual mentor can be a very important help in the spiritual journey. The guilt and shame that we seek to hide can be accepted, discussed, and healed in a situation of trust and openness. The gifts and possibilities we are not aware of can be pointed out. Encouragement when life is tough can be very important. Most of all, the grace of God, which we seem to forget again and again, is the most important theme of conversations on one's spiritual journey.

The "soul friend" or "spiritual director" can be a specially trained counselor or more informally a respected friend. Many spiritual directors see their clients about every three weeks. Some receive a fee for their work, while others do not. Serving as a companion to another wayfarer is holy work and is especially gratifying when the discernment of God's grace in the person's life brings new spiritual fruit.

• AIDS FOR THE EXERCISES

Baldwin, Christina. *Life's Companion: Journal Writing as a Spiritual Quest.* New York: Bantam, 1990.

Edwards, Tilden. *Spiritual Friend.* New York: Paulist, 1980.

Klug, Ronald. *How to Keep a Spiritual Journal.* Minneapolis: Augsburg, 1993.

Leech, Kenneth. *Soul Friend: The Practice of Christian Spirituality.* San Francisco: Harper & Row, 1980.

Sellner, Edward C. *Mentoring: The Ministry of Spiritual Kinship.* Notre Dame, Ind.: Ave Maria, 1990.

• SUGGESTED READING

Anonymous. *The Way of a Pilgrim and The Pilgrim Continues His Way.* Trans. R. M. French. New York: Seabury, 1952.

Bosch, David J. *Transforming Mission: Paradigm Shifts in Theology of Mission.* Maryknoll, N.Y.: Orbis, 1991.

Erb, Peter C., ed. *The Pietists: Selected Writings.* Classics of Western Spirituality Series. New York: Paulist, 1983.

Francis de Sales. *Introduction to the Devout Life.* Garden City, N.Y.: Image Books, 1972.

Fremantle, Anne, ed. *The Protestant Mystics.* New York: New American Library, 1964.

Madame Guyon: An Autobiography. Chicago: Moody, n.d.

Spener, Philip Jacob. *Pia Desideria.* Minneapolis: Fortress, 1989 (1964).

Steere, Douglas V., ed. *Quaker Spirituality: Selected Writings.* Classics of Western Spirituality Series. New York: Paulist, 1984.

7 | *The Twentieth Century*

As we approach the end of the twentieth century, its beginnings seem far in the past. So much has changed in so few decades. In Europe and America we have gone from optimism to despair and back several times. We have been disillusioned by two world wars and a great depression. We have seen the horrors of Auschwitz and Hiroshima, we have heard of Stalin's genocide in the Ukraine. We have lived under the mushroom cloud and have seen the Soviet Union rise and fall. We have traveled to the moon and have seen the beauty of the earth from space. It is a beauty we now perceive to be threatened by ecological disaster. In the twentieth century the population of the earth has increased fourfold, along with hunger, malnutrition, and poverty. Christianity has spread to about one-third of the human population, making its biggest gains this century in Africa.[1]

A new consciousness has been emerging in this century. We are looking at reason and science with more nuanced valuation. We are struggling to find new gender balance in our understanding, new psychological appreciation for the depths of the human, introduced to us by Freud, Jung, and others.

The churches of the world have developed new ecumenical relationships since a famous meeting of missionaries in 1910 in Edinburgh. Now the World Council of Churches is almost a half-century old. The Roman Catholic Church has changed since the Second Vatican Council in the 1960s from monolithic isolation to dialogue with other Christians, with modern society, and with other religions.

We live in a world much more closely connected by communications media and by economic interdependence than the world at the start of the century. But we have not made very much progress toward eliminating war or poverty. The Arab-Israeli dispute continues. South Africa lurches toward a nonracial democracy, but progress is continually hindered by new rounds of blood-letting. African populations throughout the continent are stirring for more democracy after almost a half-century of independent, but authoritarian, governments.

The challenges Christians face at this time are immensely complex, but many of them are the same fundamental problems faced throughout the history of the faith. How are we to "mend" a creation that is ripped and torn? How are we to live faithfully before a holy God who redeems and sanctifies us? How shall we face the continuing threats of the powers of evil and the heavy weight of personal and communal guilt? How are we to build community, proclaim the gospel, and protect those at the margins of society from injustice, disease, and illiteracy? What does it mean concretely for us to live to the glory of God?

A number of movements and individuals have addressed these and newer issues in our century. I will describe a small sample. The number of people to choose from seems to grow geometrically as we come closer to our own time. I will include first two major movements that have affected all continents, then a few samples from each continent.

The Charismatic Dimension Reemerged

Pentecostalism was consciously founded as a reenactment of early Christianity as seen in the Acts of the Apostles. The experience of the earliest church seemed to contrast greatly with what was observed in twentieth-century churches. This was not the first or the last attempt to recapture the harmony and power of primitive Christianity. For example, the Restorationist Movement of the past century in the United States had led the Disciples of Christ and Churches of Christ to attempt to free the church of denominationalism and to worship as the earliest Christians worshiped. The Society of Brothers, a community founded in Germany in 1920, saw the key to early Christian authenticity in the sharing of goods, pacifism, and group discipline.

The immediate antecedents of the Pentecostals were the Holiness Movements, parachurch organizations such as the Keswick Convention in Britain, which continued Wesley's teaching of entire sanctification when the Methodist Churches had lost interest in it. Many felt a longing for "something more" than the justification by grace they had experienced at conversion. They lacked the power to live the new life expected by these groups, a life of holiness, avoiding the pleasures of the world and devoting themselves to evangelism and social reform.

What was new in Pentecostalism was the identification of Wesley's "second blessing" with the biblical "baptism in/with the Holy Spirit" (see Luke 3:16; Acts 1:5). Furthermore, the outward sign of the baptism was speaking in tongues followed by the "spiritual gifts" listed by Paul in 1 Corinthians 12, among them prophecy and healing.

The pivotal moment in the development of a new style of Christian spirituality was in a store-front church on Azusa Street in Los Angeles in 1906. At that time a black evangelist, **William Seymour** (1870-1922), introduced both black and white seekers to "baptism with the Holy Spirit" and speaking in tongues. The movement spread with lightning speed and grew quickly in North and South America. Today Pentecostal denominations are said to be the fastest-growing segment of Christianity on all continents.

Earliest Pentecostalism was multiracial, but as the movement spread and solidified into denominations, black and white generally organized separately. They were despised and rejected by the established churches because they were mostly poor, uneducated people. Pentacostalists charged that the churches had lost the power of the Holy Spirit. Over the decades Pentecostalism became more moderate as its members gained in affluence, just as Wesley's followers had. They began to found colleges and build handsome churches. The more extreme emotional outbursts in services, which had led to their nickname, "Holy Rollers," were not so frequent.

Finally, they came to recognize genuine spiritual gifts in members of the so-called mainline denominations. In the 1960s and '70s large numbers of Protestants and Catholics, and even a few Orthodox Christians were led by the neo-Pentecostal or charismatic movement to the same experiences as "classical" Pentecostalism. Unlike the people affected in the first few decades of this century, these charismatics remained in their historic denominations instead of starting new ones. They did not necessarily accept the fundamentalism and the list of forbidden activities of the original Pentecostals. But they did begin to take evangelism, healing, and praise very seriously. The movement had its greatest success, surprisingly, among Roman Catholics. The hierarchy saw to it that priestly guidance was given to an essentially lay movement, which began in universities. Cardinal Suenens and Pope Paul VI blessed the movement.

The Protestant churches reacted much more cautiously and sometimes with hostility. The more conservative churches were, surprisingly, the most critical. The Lutheran Church–Missouri Synod, for example, defrocked some of its clergy for their participation. Parachurch organizations demanded signed statements from employees that they would not speak in tongues.

What is Pentecostal or charismatic spirituality? It focuses on the love of God seen to be present and active. The practice of speaking in tongues is experienced as an assurance of God's love. "Letting go" to allow the Spirit to guide the sounds from the mouth is a form of surrender to God. Answers to prayers for healing of physical or emotional problems likewise underline the presence and power of God. The Holy Spirit, brought into prominence in this movement, nevertheless takes second place to Christ as the Savior and Friend of the worshiper. The group is the locus for hearing the Word of God both through Scripture and prophecy. Prophecies are often cast in the form of the biblical prophets, e.g., "My people, hear my voice. . . ." It is understood that God is actively communicating with the group in these spontaneous messages, which are subject to the norms of Scripture and the judgment of the leadership. In this way the movement is similar to the Quaker form of worship.

The traditional suspicion of education and intellectual endeavor in the earliest Pentecostalists was not emphasized among neo-Pentecostalists, but there was still a sense that the anointing of the Spirit was more important than academic degrees for leadership. One Nigerian told me, "We don't need any more leaders with their heads full of Greek and their hearts full of lust!"

A few charismatic persons took dramatic steps to help the poor as the result of their spiritual renewal. But as a whole the movement did not make care for the poor or advocacy for the oppressed a major theme. The prophecies rarely had the authentic challenge for justice found in the Hebrew prophets, but instead focused on inner assurance of God's love or challenges to religious duties within the group. Thus the movement came in some instances to meet the real thirst of American Christians for an emotional and experiential faith, but it did not challenge their social or political involvement. The movement definitely led to ecumenical exchanges between surprising partners, notably the Pentecostals and Roman Catholics. But in some places congregations were divided.

Today thousands of Catholics and Protestants who have experienced "baptism in the Spirit" and speaking in tongues are no longer active in the charismatic movement. These people are sometimes continuing a renewed involvement in the churches and even using the gift of tongues in private devotion. They have become a hidden part of the denominations that is longing for more instruction in spirituality than the church has given.

Ecumenical Spirituality Drew
Churches Together

The movement for Christian unity known as ecumenism did not begin in the twentieth century. Ever since there have been divisions in the churches, there have been those who have prayed for reunion. For example, Philip Melanchthon, the young associate of Luther, tried hard to reconcile Lutherans with others. But in the present century ecumenism has developed not only major institutions but widespread themes for prayer among denominations.

The institutions of ecumenism include the Evangelical Alliance, the World Missionary Federation, The Faith and Order movement, the Life and Work conferences, the World Council of Churches (WCC) (1948), and others.

What is of special interest to us here is the growth of a movement of prayer for Christian unity. A week specially devoted to this cause was started in 1908, then approved by Pope Pius X in 1909. At that time many Protestants understood Roman Catholic ecumenism to mean that Protestants should "come home" to Rome. But Abbe Paul Couterier (1881-1953), who was experienced in building understanding between French Catholics and Reformed churches, was able to convince Protestants to adopt the same week, January 18-25, for the purpose of prayer for unity. Since 1966 the Vatican and the World Council of Churches have planned and promoted the Week of Prayer for Christian Unity together.

Orthodox, Catholics, and Protestants in the present century have learned to pray together on many levels at meetings, conferences, and retreats. Many believe that it is only prayer that has kept the movement going in spite of many obstacles. As yet there has been little approved sharing of Holy Communion, but a great deal of intercommunion has taken place informally.

A very special expression of ecumenical spirituality is the community of Taize in France. Founded by Roger Schutz and Max Thurien, it is a semi-monastic order with members from both Catholic and Protestant traditions. The Orthodox have also made their contribution. At a service led by Brother Roger in a packed Episcopal cathedral in Edinburgh, I watched as many non-Orthodox believers joined in kissing a large cross-shaped icon lying in the middle of the church floor as a prayer of solidarity with Russian Christians.

It could be argued that the Protestant ecumenical movement was begun by missionaries, taken over in mid-century by liberal bureaucrats, and forced to stretch in the second half of the century by third world Christians and Orthodox and Catholic partners. The presence of the Orthodox churches in the World Council was followed by Vatican II declarations on ecumenism. After the 1960s ecumenism was changed from an inter-Protestant, largely European and North American affair, into something truly ecumenical, that is worldwide.

Conservative evangelicals, long distrustful of the WCC, may never become members, but there is an increasing recognition on both sides of the need to talk instead of ignoring or vilifying each other.

The Pentecostal and ecumenical movements are truly global in influence.

As we turn now to many of the continents of the world, I want to emphasize my belief that the Western world, the so-called first world, needs the so-called third world in order to develop an authentic and vital spirituality. A very good general guide to this process is William Dyrness's book, *Learning about Theology from the Third World*.[2] His focus is on theology, but theology does overlap with Christian spirituality, and the general picture he gives is a helpful expansion of our horizons. Dyrness describes African theology as focused on Christianity and culture, Latin American theology as centering on the political setting, and Asian theology as discerning the transcendent as its main theme. These are overgeneralizations as the author realizes.

His point, however, is that Christians in the West can no longer afford to leave out of consideration the contributions and challenges of Christians from these continents. That is, these Christians have both gifts to offer from their own cultural backgrounds and hard questions to ask of the affluent Christians of the West.

More directly related to spirituality is *Common Journey, Different Paths: Spiritual Direction in Cross-Cultural Perspective*.[3] This collection of articles by spiritual directors on different continents explores the issues of multicultural communication by sharing the experiences of Catholic spiritual directors.

Whereas the numbers of Christians in Europe and North America show little increase, in the other continents Christianity is growing rapidly, and mission societies are being founded to evangelize other countries, including the West. The very vitality of these Christians is a refreshment to the tired churches in secularized, affluent countries. *Christianity Rediscovered*[4] tells of the power of a simple gospel among the Maasai in East Africa. Such rediscoveries are also needed in countries where Christianity has long been present.

Latin America

Roman Catholic Christianity came to Latin America with the conquistadors and since then has spread at least nominally to the vast majority of the population. In many countries the ordinary people did not understand the faith, and it became an overlay on their previous beliefs. Furthermore, the church came to be a bastion of support for the European populations that held and still hold the land and economic power. In some countries 2 percent of the people own 90 percent of the land. The question of social justice was muffled by the cultural captivity of the hierarchy.

But in the mid twentieth century "base Christian communities" were started, which involved the poor people in Bible-based group meetings that enlivened faith and called into question the economic order. The camposinos, or peasants, learned to read and to think critically about their lives. This grassroots movement is what gave birth to a new kind of theology, liberation theology.

Liberation theology eventually was adopted by professional theologians and is now well known throughout the world. It advocates a new way of doing theology, from the perspective of the poor, from the "bottom up." It employs Marxist analysis to reveal the injustice and conflict in the human situation, then the Christian gospel to promise hope for liberation from oppression in the historical future. This theology has been criticized from both Catholic and Protestant conservative perspectives on a number of accounts. It has seemed to some to tend toward a secular theology of social and economic revolution without any transcendent or specifically spiritual content.

Gustavo Gutierrez (b. 1928), in *We Drink from Our Own Wells*, describes a liberation spirituality that must give the critics pause. His book is valuable in many ways. On the basis of the Latin American poor, he finds traditional Catholic spirituality to fall short on two counts: it is geared to a minority, namely the religious orders, and it is too individualistic and interior. What is needed is a spirituality for all the people that includes practical action for liberation on a communal level. Drawing on the Bible and on selected figures from the history of European spirituality, Gutierrez calls for a wholistic view of the Christian life, consisting of a Trinitarian "Encounter with the Lord, Walking in the Spirit, and a Journey to the Father." See Gutierrez on p. 141 in the Bibliography.

For Protestants, one of the attractive features of the book is the seriousness with which Gutierrez takes the Bible. In the course of his discussion he also deals at length with Paul's understanding of flesh, spirit, and body. He shows that Paul is not following Neo-Platonist denigration of the body, but is using the term *flesh* in a different sense. This section would be helpful in many books on spirituality, and it is unfortunate that these findings of critical word study were not available centuries earlier.

The special marks of liberation spirituality as set forth in this book are conversion (the necessary break with the past, which occurs again and again), gratuitousness (the free, unearned grace of God), joy in suffering and martyrdom (which come in the struggle for liberation), spiritual childhood (which he sees as necessary for a commitment to the poor), and community (as the proper context for solitude).

The problematic elements of liberation theology hardly appear in Gutierrez's book. There is nothing of Marxist analysis here. It is clear that spirituality is for personal and communal relationship to God and not simply for political revolution. Gutierrez is known as a theologian who lives simply among the people, practicing what he advocates in his writing. Similar in tone is Jon Sobrino's *Spirituality of Liberation*.[5] This book is a fresh and serious challenge to others in their own settings to rethink spirituality on biblical, liberationist lines.

The challenge of liberation spirituality for North Americans is twofold. Is our spirituality so individualized and psychologized that it excludes issues of justice? Are we prepared to share power with groups that have been disempowered, either within our own societies or in the two-thirds world?

Africa

There are two main developments in African spirituality that I would raise for your consideration: the first, liberation concepts in the African setting, and the second, the movement to contextualize African Christianity.

The first movement finds a very similar expression to that of Gutierrez in the volume by Archbishop **Bakole Wa Ilunga**, *Paths of Liberation: A Third World Spirituality*. Both are Catholic authors who in the post-Vatican II setting give considerable attention to the Bible. Both are proposing serious changes for their countries on the basis of experience of oppression and the longing for freedom. Ilunga expresses the essence of freedom as that which enhances life, a central theme in many accounts of African traditions.

The first third of Ilunga's book is a frank discussion of the problems of Zaire, in central Africa. He not only decries the damage to his people brought by years of colonial alienation and present foreign manipulation, but lays out the responsibility of present-day Zaireans for the crushing poverty of the country. President Mobutu's policy of "Authenticity" is criticized for not leading back to true African roots, but becoming a political shibboleth behind which all sorts of schemes to defraud people can succeed. The growth of government corruption leading to paralysis of the economy is frankly described, both on high and low levels. The root problem, Ilunga concludes, is human sin: "the underlying cause of all the things that do not work."[6]

Ilunga's prescription, based on a lengthy discussion of the Bible, is that personal liberation must go hand in hand with social, political liberation. If individuals are not freed from sin, even the most just system will not liberate the poor.

Under the banner of black theology, significant development of the liberation theme has also taken place in southern Africa. The black theology and black consciousness movements in tandem with similar movements in the United States have articulated a theological opposition to the apartheid system. This system has roots far back in the immigration of Europeans to South Africa since 1652. It was codified into law following the victory of the Nationalist Party in 1948. *Apartheid* is an Afrikaans word that means "separateness." Although supported by the Dutch Reformed Church in South Africa, it was clear to all others, especially the nonwhite population that suffers under this system, that it was unjust, immoral, and sinful. The churches of English background spoke up against apartheid from the beginning but were unable to take decisive action against it. These churches, whose members are mostly black, nevertheless include many white people of British descent whose economic interests led them to support apartheid at the polls while condemning it in church resolutions.[7]

Some courageous individuals have opposed the system, such as Alan Paton, whose novels, beginning with *Cry, the Beloved Country*, describe the pain and suffering caused by the system. Deeply Christian, Paton's vision is one of deep compassion for all sides. Paton comes from the British side of the white population. From the Afrikaner side, no one has been better known than Beyers Naude, who suffered rejection by the Dutch Reformed Church and eventually banning (house arrest) by the South African government.

Apartheid lost ground in the days following the release of Nelson Mandela. The laws that codified it in the 1950s were rescinded, and the prisoners and exiles returned. But as I write the apartheid system continues in effect because there is no vote yet for the black population, and radical whites are stirring up violence in the townships and bantustans where the black population has been forced to live. In this situation of uncertainty, hope, and fear, both black and white Christians are praying that their country will emerge as a multiracial democracy where human rights are honored.

John de Gruchy has gathered an engaging, challenging collection of South African spiritual writings under the title *Cry Justice!*[8] He is another of the courageous Afrikaners who have broken with apartheid. A special characteristic of this daily devotional guide is the inclusion of songs and artwork as well as prayers and meditations from South African Christians. This little book illustrates the wide variety of material that expresses and shapes spirituality while keeping the social justice dimension in the context of the message of the grace of God.

The book contains the music and words for the powerful hymn, "Nkosi Sikele' iAfrika," which is sung all over southern Africa. Composed by Enoch Sontonga in the Xhosa language at a Methodist mission school in 1897, it was adopted as the official anthem of the African National Congress in 1912. I have always been deeply moved when I have heard this anthem. Here is an English translation:

> Lord, in your mercy bless Africa.
> Lift up the horn of her power and strength.
> In your love and kindness hear our prayer,
> Father look on us, and bless your family.
> Come, Spirit come—come and bless us
> Come, Spirit come—come and bless us
> Father, look down, and bless Africa,
> Father look on us, and bless your family.[9]

The most well known of the Christian opponents of apartheid is **Desmond Tutu** (b. 1931), archbishop of Johannesburg and winner of the Nobel Peace Prize. He is the author of a number of short books containing sermons and meditations, appealing for both justice and reconciliation. Tutu is known not only for leading marches and conducting mass funerals for the victims of apartheid, but also for his spiritual leadership. He is known to be a person of prayer, rising very early each morning to spend an hour or more with God.

Namibia, which borders South Africa on the northwest, was under the heel of the South African apartheid system until March of 1990. Lutheran pastor **Zephania Kameeta**, who since independence has been elected a leader in the Namibian Parliament, published a book of prayers in the midst of oppression, *Why, O Lord?* The book introduces the Namibian situation, then includes meditations and paraphrases of Scripture. For example, Psalm 27 begins,

> The Lord is my light and my liberation;
> I will fear no so-called world powers.
> The Lord protects me from all danger;
> I will never be afraid.

When their "security forces" attack me
and try to kill me,
they stumble and fall.
Even if their whole imperialist armies surround me,
I will not be afraid;
I will still trust in God my Liberator.[10]

These poems give sharp expression to the oppression experienced by black Namibians.

The second main theme in African Christian spirituality is contextualization. What will a Christianity that is fully African look like? The quest for an indigenous cultural expression of Christianity has led to a reevaluation of the primal religions and new interest in the ancient African churches of Egypt and Ethiopia, together with careful study of the so-called African Independent churches.

Missionaries from the North Atlantic countries generally taught Christianity on the basis of their own post-Enlightenment, modern assumptions and addressed their answers to the kinds of questions they were accustomed to at home. Christianity became a classroom religion for many people. It taught reading and writing and the correct answers to the questions in the catechism, whether Catholic, Reformed, or Lutheran, but it often did not address the questions Africans raised.

Christianity was attractive to Africans because of the prestige of a Scripture, the possibility of confidence in the love of the Creator, and the promise of secure and eternal life after death. But post-Enlightenment missionary Christianity did not have much to say about issues of daily concern: the status of the ancestors; the role of spirits and divinities; contact with the unseen world through visions, dreams, and animals; and especially matters of health and fertility. These issues had already been secularized in Europe and North America, and missionaries became the agents of secularization in Africa, knowingly or unknowingly.

This contrast became vividly apparent in the ministry of **William Wade Harris** (1866-1929).[11] A forty-seven-year-old Liberian, Harris was called while in prison to be a prophet. He discarded all Western clothing and set off walking near the Atlantic across Ivory Coast, preaching to indigenous peoples that they should abandon their old gods and be baptized in the name of the Father, Son, and Holy Spirit. There had been a few missionaries in Ivory Coast for about twenty years, but they had found little success in convincing people of a "modern" worldview. Harris, however, spoke to the people within their own worldview. Like them he believed in the power of their gods and spirits and in the possibility of miracles. His demonstration of "signs and wonders" like those in the Acts of the Apostles convinced many people to burn their old images and amulets and to be baptized by Harris. Unlike the missionaries, he did not demand any book learning before baptism. By baptism people felt immediately defended from the revenge of their abandoned gods by the spiritual power of the new God, who loved them. Harris was not concerned about denominations. Some of those baptized by him became Catholic, others Methodist, and still others started indigenous churches. Harris walked all the way to Gold Coast (now Ghana) and back across Ivory Coast to Liberia in the years 1913-15. It is said that more than 100,000 people responded to this African prophet, with his bamboo cross, turban and robe, calabash rattle, and bowl of baptismal water! He kept the local communities together instead of separating out individual converts as the European missionaries did. He also permitted and practiced polygamy, a traditional form of African marriage.

The example of the prophet Harris is not unique. Other African prophets emerged in our century: Garrick Braide in Nigeria, Simon Kimbangu in Zaire, and many others. None of them set out deliberately to "accommodate" Christianity to African culture, but all of them did an "end run" around Western ideas of Christianity. In seeking to be faithful to the Bible and to the Spirit, they did produce a form of Christianity that was indigenous to Africa, a "contextualized" faith. The churches founded by these prophets and others are commonly called "African Indigenous Churches" and are now looked upon as providing clues for the contextualization of spirituality in the mission-founded churches.

They portend a special type of spirituality that is strange to the European individualist, rationalist spirituality of recent centuries. The major themes are the affirmation of life in this world as well as beyond the grave, the role of the living dead in the communion of saints, the importance of healing, and the presence of the Spirit to work in power. Some of these themes are found in Pentecostal Christianity on all continents; others are distinctive to Africa.

African Christianity has both gifts and challenges for first-world Christians. I see the gifts as (1) a sense of the presence of God in all things, (2) an experience of the Spirit of God for power to meet the challenges of life, (3) a strong emphasis on the community, and (4) the eagerness to celebrate in music and dance the glory of God. The challenge on the other hand comes from the racially troubled southern region of Africa, where race relations bear some marks of the North American racial atmosphere. It is easy for foreigners to condemn apartheid in South Africa if it does not cost anything to do so; it is much more challenging to change American society so that it will be racially just. Both Native Americans and African Americans have suffered here under European American domination.

Asia

The world's largest continent also has the most people but the smallest percentage of Christians. Though Christianity began in western Asia, its thought forms seem quite different from those of the ancient civilizations of India and

China. On this continent lie some of the most difficult cultural challenges to an indigenous Christian spirituality. As with the other continents, I will not attempt any sort of completeness in this discussion but will select a few highlights.

No one who has read **Kosuke Koyama**'s (b. 1929) whirlwind theological tour of Asia can assume that Asia has the same cultural similarity as the peoples of Africa. His *Waterbuffalo Theology* hints at the very different situations in Singapore, Thailand, China, Hong Kong, the Philippines, Indonesia, Burma, Vietnam, Japan, and Taiwan. In the situation of northern Thailand where he is writing, he speaks of a "monsoon orientation" as "cyclical cosmic regularity and its saving dependability without hurry and without argument."[12] How different from the spirit of the industrialized countries, including his own homeland, Japan! This difference is indicated in the meditations he titles *Three Mile an Hour God*.[13] Koyama is intensely aware of the cultural differences within Asia as well as those between Asia and the West. His conversational style, freehand drawings, and witty remarks show a down-to-earth spirituality.

Koyama calls for quite a different direction in spirituality from the Latin American and African sources we have discussed. This is not a spirituality of social justice or of contextualization, but a spirituality of the cross, as the place where a God of history expresses wrath about human sin. Koyama is not trying to blend together Asian religions and Christianity, but is focusing on the very stumbling block that Paul wrote about—the cross. In his *No Handle on the Cross*, Koyama rejects human attempts to control God or to reduce the offensiveness of the Christian message by taking the spotlight off of the cross of Jesus. Koyama is very sensitive to the presence of idolatry of various kinds, and he writes about it in *Mount Fuji and Mount Sinai*.[14]

Sometimes Koyama sounds very much like Luther's "theology of the cross" as opposed to a "theology of glory." (See p. 71.)

In India, we see a development outwardly similar to African contextualization but quite different in content. The development of a friendly Christian relationship to Hinduism goes in the direction of a mysticism not characteristic of Africa. Drawing on the resources of Ramanuja, Sadhu Sundar Singh, and Krishna Pillai, **A. J. Appasamy** developed a Christian spirituality in the *bhakti* tradition of Hinduism. *Bhakti* refers to the way of salvation by devotion rather than by the other two major paths in Hinduism: knowledge and moral achievement. It is the path that seems to be the closest to the Christian concept of salvation by grace. Starting from his doctoral dissertation at Oxford, Appasamy related the message of the Gospel of John to Indian mysticism. He was friendly to the use of Hindu terminology and practice.

I must also mention the Albanian nun who has become known worldwide for her work among the sick and dying in Calcutta. **Mother Teresa** (b. 1910) no longer belongs to any particular continent, as the work of her order now circles the globe. Her spirituality is simple and biblical: she sees Christ in the suffering persons she helps (Matthew 25). She insists that her sisters take their prayer and worship lives very seriously, or they will burn out in serving the poorest of the poor. This profound simplicity has become a Christian witness to Christians and non-Christians alike. Mother Teresa has combined a fearless confrontation with traditional customs and government authorities with a savvy ability to get things done. Yet she attends daily mass as an essential part of her day.

We cannot all be Mother Teresas, yet the wholism of her spirituality is worthy of emulation: prayer and work go together.

Other developments in Asia include the surprising emergence of the Christian church in China after decades of repression, the Minjung theology of Korea, the Christian dialogue with Buddhism in Japan, and the quests for indigenization in the southern islands such as Papua New Guinea.

Europe

The continent seen to be most Christian in previous centuries has had a difficult time in the twentieth century. The optimism of the first decade was shattered by World War I; the Depression of the thirties and World War II devastated the continent. The horrors of the Holocaust, the growth of Marxist atheism, secularism, and many intellectual challenges to the truth of Christianity have left a continent nominally Christian, with only a remnant serious about Christian spirituality. Yet that remnant has been both innovative and devoted to the study of the tradition.

Among the many twentieth-century writers on mysticism, perhaps the most influential in the English-speaking world was **Evelyn Underhill** (1875-1941). She became a mystic in the philosophical, Platonic sense before being baptized as a Christian in adulthood. The person who influenced her most became her spiritual director: Baron Friedrich von Hügel. He was a modernist Roman Catholic lay theologian living in England.

Underhill is known for her major study, *Mysticism*, first published in 1911, and her later *Worship* of 1936. She drew the attention of many people to the classical mystical texts. She devoted herself to a ministry of personal spiritual direction from her home and also led retreats. Underhill's interest in spirituality and mysticism was not merely academic; she was actively involved with the practical problems of real people.

On the continent, one of the outstanding Christian theologians and martyrs was **Dietrich Bonhoeffer** (1906-45). He first became widely known for his provocative commentary on the Sermon on the Mount, *The Cost of Discipleship*. Like Kierkegaard almost a century earlier, he castigated his own Lutheran tradition for preaching "cheap grace," an easy, uninvolved Christianity. The whole nation, he said, had been baptized with little sense of the meaning of being Jesus' disciple.

Later Bonhoeffer became known as a martyr after his execution by the Nazis five days before the Americans liberated his prison. He had been arrested for his role in plotting the assassination of Hitler. Once he had been safe in New York, but he felt he had to return to Germany to fight Hitler. While he was there he taught at a secret seminary in Finkenwalde, where he gave spiritual direction to the students and wrote *Life Together*, which describes the basis of Christian community. It also describes his advice for reading Scripture and for meditation.

Some have come to know Bonhoeffer exclusively through *Letters and Papers from Prison*, published after his death by his friend Eberhard Bethge. The letters introduced phrases much used in 1960s theology: "religionless Christianity," "secular holiness," and "man come of age." He was critical of religion as a replacement for the living God, and he decried the "God of the gaps," a God who was only used to explain what science did not yet explain. Some people took his book as the banner of a politicized Christianity, leaving out traditional spirituality altogether. Since that time, more balance has come in the interpretation of Bonhoeffer, and he may well be one of the theologians and spiritual writers who is remembered into the next century.

In the Orthodox world, the twentieth century has seen great suffering under the Bolshevik regimes, especially that of Stalin. But there is a new freedom for spiritual pursuits since the Soviet Union disintegrated. The revival of what is old has marked the Orthodox tradition again and again through the centuries. In the twentieth century, hesychasm, the *Philokalia*, *The Way of a Pilgrim*, and movements among the Russian intellectuals have again revived what is old. Beyond the Eastern European countries where Orthodoxy is strong, there has been impressive growth in western Europe and North America, where emigres have come to live, pray, and study. The translation into English of Orthodox works is having significant impact on Catholics and Protestants. Especially the Anglican communion has seen its calling as a bridge between East and West.

North America

Finally we come to our own continent, where we have experienced great gains in material prosperity in this century, and in spite of participating in many wars, have not suffered from them on our own ground. Yet the inequalities in the societies of Canada and the United States and the continuing hunger for genuine spiritual nourishment are very real.

One of the outstanding figures in Christian spirituality of our century was **Thomas Merton** (1915-68). He was born in France of parents from New Zealand and the United States. He spent most of his childhood in Europe, where he mastered several languages. By the time he entered Columbia University in New York, he was already writing a great deal. His conversion to Catholicism and quick entrance into a monastery were shocking to some of his friends but were somewhat parallel to the changes in Augustine's life fifteen hundred years earlier. Like Augustine's *Confessions,* Merton's *Seven Storey Mountain* told his inner autobiography. Merton's book became a best-seller and made his name well known in the Christian world.

Merton entered the Trappist monastery of Our Lady of Gethsemani, Kentucky, in 1941. The Trappists are one of the strictest branches of Catholic monks. They continue to practice the full seven traditional prayer times each day and to follow a vow of silence, not speaking to each other except for limited occasions. It is a life following the Benedictine Rule, with manual labor, prayer, and sacred reading. The success of Merton's autobiography and subsequent books eventually produced the major part of the monastery's income.

Merton loved the contemplative life, but he also hated certain aspects of it. He was in friction with the abbot over the rules of enclosure and how to deal with his writings. But he would not have developed into the writer he did without the monastic life. He was told to write about early monastic saints and translate their writings. This led him to become an expert on monastic history, not only of his own order, but of all monasticism, going back to the Egyptian hermits.

Eventually Merton himself wanted the solitude of the hermit. After a long period of requests, the order agreed to approve the practice of hermitage for some stable monks, and Merton was given permission. He had his own house, called Our Lady of Carmel.

Early in his career, Merton was enthusiastic about the writings of John of the Cross and Teresa of Avila. Later he came to love Mother Julian of Norwich even more.

Merton's interest in Asian religion was roused in the 1960s, and he explored the relations between Christian and Buddhist meditation. He died tragically in an electrical accident at a conference in Bangkok, Thailand, in 1968.

Merton brought a renewal of monastic life not only to his monastery and his order, but also to seekers everywhere. He did not really break new ground but revived the old, applying it to new problems. He stands as a witness for the contemplative life as a genuine Christian calling, without any "social utility." He believed a life of contemplative prayer was worthwhile without any social works to justify it. But he was very much interested in social problems and was a strong advocate for peace.

In late life Merton also entered into dialogue with people of other faiths. He did not leave Christianity behind but explored what Buddhists and Christians could learn from each other.

A similar question is being raised by many North Americans about the relation of Christianity to Native American cultures and religions. Many American Indians and a number of non-Indians are thinking deeply about the relationship between Christianity and the religions of Native Americans. Many are asking if the commonalities of these two have been overlooked. Others are calling for a Native American spirituality within Christianity. Especially attractive are the traditional Indian reverence for "all one's relatives" (all living creatures and even all things in nature) and the honored roles for women. Many Native Americans are Christian and are seeking a spirituality that will combine their traditions with the gospel of Jesus.

The African-American population is overwhelmingly Christian and has been nourished down through the centuries by a spirituality of endurance, liberation, and celebration. African-Americans have suffered unspeakably from slavery and then discrimination. Those sufferings have produced a community drawn together in worship that reaches the heart. James Cone, who earlier wrote hard-hitting books of black liberation theology, has turned in recent years to an analysis of the spirituality of the black church. He sees in the music and preaching of the Christian community the core of values that has sustained African-Americans.

Martin Luther King, Jr. (1929-68) is the best known of African-Americans throughout the world. It is significant that the civil rights leader was also a Baptist preacher. His vision of the mountain the night before his death testifies to spiritual roots that sustained his quest for justice through militant nonviolence. His *Letter from a Birmingham Jail,* explaining why he chose to break the law for the sake of justice, and *Strength to Love,* indicating the spiritual basis for a long-term struggle, both testify to a spirituality that was expressed in his public actions.

As we approach the end of the century, four developments in American spirituality call for special comment: (1) the influence of psychology, (2) women's and men's spirituality, (3) Twelve-Step spirituality, and (4) creation-centered spirituality.

1. The world of thought in which spirituality has developed in North America has been deeply influenced by the relatively new discipline of psychology. Perhaps more than any other continent, we seek self-fulfillment, self-realization, and mental health through our spiritualities. This point underlies all four of the movements on this list along with many others.

On the one hand, I see this as a positive "contextualizing" of the gospel in America. Christians seek to meet people where they are hurting. The theme of healing is a very important one to many of us as we think of Christian spirituality. The charismatic Catholic Francis MacNutt has written helpful works on this theme, as has the trio of Matt and Dennis Linn and Sheila Fabricant Linn. Episcopalian Morton Kelsey has written prolifically on healing, dreams, speaking in tongues, and other themes. All of these writers describe "inner healing" of emotional wounds from childhood. This is a new approach in the history of Christian spirituality, which has been influenced by psychologists. It is a very helpful approach in my opinion.

A number of major writers on spirituality base their understanding of the human mind on the work of Karl Jung. Jung was friendlier to Christianity than was Freud, but others think that his viewpoint distorts the Christian message and that Freud or someone more recent would be a better basis. The Meyers-Briggs Type Indicator has its roots in Jung. A number of books describe connections between learning one's type and helpful spiritual practices.

On the other hand, the influence of psychology has been limiting. It can produce a self-absorption that is blind to social justice and ecological balance. If all I want is mental health, I will seek what I can get out of Christian spirituality, but I will not have it in balance. If we listen to the Latin Americans, the Africans, and the Asians, we will be encouraged to see the power of God in healing individuals, but we will not be allowed to stop there. Our neighbors will force us to consider all four of the dimensions of spirituality and not just to be absorbed in ourselves.

2. Western churches are in the midst of a serious reevaluation of their spiritual roots in response to the new consciousness among women. In the United States, the radical feminism of the few in the '70s has developed into a more widespread women's movement in the churches and is influencing not just personnel policies and the language of hymns, but also the way we think about God. Women's Christian spirituality has become a source of renewal.

Much of the history of Christian spirituality, with some notable exceptions, has been developed and reported by men. The question that is being asked is whether a thoroughgoing change in tone is needed so that the concerns of women are also addressed. Among these are the way in which Christians image God. If God is uniformly referred to with male metaphors such as Father, Lord, and King, and the male pronoun is always used, then it is difficult to see how women are made in the image of God. The biblical and historical witness to a variety of images for God has many times been lost in popular piety, leaving many women alienated.

Another concern is the view of the body and sexuality in Christian spirituality. The tradition has had large numbers of celibate men as leading teachers. These men did not have a balanced view of the goodness of sex as God's creation. Women appeared to them as temptations to sin. Even noncelibate men have looked upon women more as sex objects, and therefore temptresses, than as partners in the spiritual life.

A fresh view of the relation of the sexes in spirituality is emerging, in which the female as well as male character of God is recognized, and the gifts of women are recognized along with those of men. The experiences and views of men should not be the norm; women's views and experiences are fully as important.

Two kinds of writers of women's spirituality have emerged. One type wishes to remain within the Christian tradition, reforming it to avoid dualisms and hierarchies and to highly value experience, especially the experiences of women, including women from other cultures. This means reading the Bible with different eyes, looking for the women and asking how it looked from their point of view. It also means being skeptical of the Christian tradition as a whole, looking for obvious and not-so-obvious ways in which males have undermined Paul's assertion that in Christ Jesus "there is no longer male and female" (Gal. 3:28).

A second kind of women's spirituality has left Christianity behind. Finding the Bible and the theological tradition of the churches just too patriarchal, a number of women have started their own spiritual groups. Some of them worship the Mother Goddess of older religions, some practice a modern revision of witchcraft, but others simply look for healing ideas, including New Age materials.

Recently a number of books have addressed a specifically masculine spirituality. Among men who view the women's movement positively and do not wish to return to patriarchal ways there is an interest in how male sexuality can be a positive element in Christian spirituality.

3. A dialogue between Twelve-Step programs and Christian spirituality is under way. Alcoholics Anonymous (AA) was founded in the United States in the 1930s by two men, "Bill W. and Dr. Bob" (William Wilson [1895-1971] and Robert Smith [1879-1950]), who were deeply influenced by the Oxford Group, later known as Moral Rearmament.[15] A thorough discussion of the influences that shaped AA indicates both Christian and secular movements.[16] They and other alcoholics were often turned off by the churches and conventional Christianity, but they deeply believed in the message of the gospel. They developed groups for alcoholics that accepted all people as the churches rarely did. Here are the Twelve Steps they developed based in part on the eight principles of the Oxford Group:

1. We admitted we were powerless over alcohol—that our lives had become unmanageable.
2. Came to believe that a Power greater than ourselves could restore us to sanity.
3. Made a decision to turn our will and our lives over to the care of God *as we understood Him.*
4. Made a searching and fearless moral inventory of ourselves.
5. Admitted to God, to ourselves, and to another human being the exact nature of our wrongs.
6. Were entirely ready to have God remove all these defects of character.
7. Humbly asked Him to remove our shortcomings.
8. Made a list of all persons we had harmed, and became willing to make amends to them all.

9. Made direct amends to such people wherever possible, except when to do so would injure them or others.
10. Continued to take personal inventory and when we were wrong promptly admitted it.
11. Sought through prayer and meditation to improve our conscious contact with God *as we understand Him,* praying only for knowledge of His will for us and the power to carry that out.
12. Having had a spiritual awakening as the result of these steps, we tried to carry this message to alcoholics, and to practice these principles in all our affairs.[17]

These steps obviously include wisdom from the tradition of Christian spirituality. Some have found these steps in the Bible as a whole[18] or in the Beatitudes from the Sermon on the Mount (Matthew 5). Nevertheless, the authors felt it necessary to expand the concept of God into what is commonly called one's "Higher Power," since many alcoholics could not relate to the usual picture of God.

Eventually over the years, the original Twelve Steps have been supplemented by a literature incorporating basic attitudes, prayer, and meditation. One of the most widely used texts in the spirituality of AA is the "Serenity Prayer," which is the first part of a longer prayer composed by theologian Reinhold Niebuhr:

God grant me the grace to accept with serenity the things I cannot change,
courage to change the things I can, and wisdom to know the difference,
living one day at a time, enjoying one moment at a time;
accepting hardship as the pathway to peace,
taking as you did this sinful world as it is, not as I would have it;
trusting that you will make all things right, if I surrender to your will;
that I may be reasonably happy in this life,
and supremely happy with you forever in the next. Amen.[19]

In recent decades this literature has increasingly caught the attention of Christian spiritual directors and pastors. Perhaps there is the possibility of more cooperation between the churches and AA.

One of the elements in this interest is the insight about the ubiquitous nature of addiction.[20] That is, what AA pioneered for one kind of addiction is relevant for others, and not only the obvious ones like drugs, gambling, and overeating. It turns out that the compulsive behaviors we find in ourselves we do not consciously choose; they relate to Paul's lament in Romans, "I do not do the good I want, but the evil I do not want is what I do" (Rom. 7:19).

The Twelve Steps are a program that includes several features of earlier spirituality, such as having a soul friend, doing a daily examen, making restitution, surrendering to God, and sharing one's belief with others. This program focuses on the discovery and overcoming of irrational, harmful habits that have at their root the insistence that "I am God." The root of addiction is seen to be spiritual, and healing begins by surrender to grace, the gift of God.

The combination of the Twelve Steps, the regular group meetings, and the personal mentor provide a powerful program for spiritual change, one that I think is of great potential value for church members.

4. Finally, I would like to discuss "creation-centered spirituality," as developed by Matthew Fox (b. 1940). He is a Dominican priest with a doctorate in spirituality who has developed both a center for developing and practicing his insights and a series of books. He knows the history of Christian spirituality very well and has developed a sharp critique of it. Fox distinguishes between the creation theme and the fall-redemption theme in Christianity. He judges that only the first is valid, and he bases his teaching on it. The fourteen themes of creation spirituality as he summarizes it include among others the creative Word of God; original blessing (instead of original sin); the celebration of all beings; the unknown, unnameable God who is a non-God; the divinization and deification of humanity; spirituality as a spiral growth process; compassion and justice; Jesus as a reminder of what it means to be God's child; and finally, laughter, newness, and joy, an affirmation of pleasure.[21] Further, he affirms panentheism, the view that all things are in God, and realized eschatology, which he defines as eternal life beginning now.

Fox writes, "We have often been fed introverted, anti-artistic, anti-intellectual, apolitical, sentimental, dualistic, ascetic and in many ways masochistic spirituality parading as Christian spirituality."[22] He sees these things in the fall-redemption spirituality which he distinguishes from creation spirituality. He is especially critical of Augustine and of the classic reformers, Luther and Calvin.

On the other hand, Fox especially likes Meister Eckhart (see pp. 62-63) and finds creation spirituality also in Benedict, Pelagius, Hildegard, Francis, Thomas, Mechtild, Julian, John of the Cross, George Fox, Rosemary Reuther, and Jon Sobrino.[23]

Fox's spirituality has many features that are attractive to me. He takes the Christian tradition seriously yet uses clear criteria to distinguish the wheat from the chaff. He uses his knowledge of the tradition to critique the tradition. He takes seriously the ecological and political dimensions of spirituality. His insights into the creative process are refreshing, and his affirmation of pleasure is needed.

Yet it seems that Fox has thrown out a vital part of Christian spirituality by discarding the fall-redemption theme. How can he separate creation and redemption so absolutely? These are themes that belong together. It is a central point of Christian praise and spiritual energy that God has forgiven our sin through the death and resurrection of Jesus. Fox seems to reject the very center of Christian belief in his version of creation spirituality.

As we come to the close of the twentieth century, many types of spirituality are available. Some of them ignore the Christian tradition, others seek to develop it. The wise person will carefully weigh the biblical message and the tradition in making choices but will be open to new perspectives from other continents as well as from recent writers. Among many such writers, too numerous to mention here, Henri Nouwen and Richard Foster have been very accessible and helpful to me. Neither one has founded a "school," but both draw selectively on the Christian tradition to make contemporary observations that reach the heart.

• DISCUSSION QUESTIONS

1. Which events of the twentieth century do you think are most important for spirituality?

2. Have you known personally a person of faith from another continent? What have you learned from the relationship?

3. What is the potential for application of liberation themes in spirituality on each of the continents?

4. What is your experience with Pentecostal or ecumenical spirituality?

5. Do you find feminist and Twelve-Step spirituality meaningful? Why or why not?

• EXERCISES: Simple Living and Writing a Letter

1. Simple living means consuming less in order to share more. It means not rushing to jam as much activity into each hour as possible. It means not wasting energy or food or possessions so as to live in better harmony with the earth. For most North Americans, following such a simple life-style would involve fundamental changes in daily life. Doing so is a matter of a process, not an absolute.

Begin by identifying one aspect of your life that could be "simplified." Sometimes it is in fact more complicated to recycle than to throw away, to repair than to replace, to bicycle than to drive. Finding ways to cut your own and your household's consumption and waste is nevertheless a worthwhile project. Start with only one part of your life-style before taking on the whole.

How you spend your money is a very important part of your spirituality. Giving away a significant fraction of your income to spiritual communities and to those in need is a practical sign of your spiritual commitment.

"Spending" time is also a sign of what you value most. Think through the times you have spun your wheels by rushing about, and see if there is a way to go at life more calmly. Taking time for the sky, the grass, and people who are important to you is part of a simple life-style.

2. In our day when citizens of democratic states have influence on national policies, writing letters can be an important spiritual exercise. Advocating the rights of those who have been denied is being a kind of preventive "good Samaritan." For example,

Bread for the World acts as an advocate for the hungry both in the United States and globally. Amnesty International works for prisoners of conscience who are often tortured or who have "disappeared." The Children's Defense Fund stands for the rights of the young. Writing letters is an effective way to stand up for justice and love in our world of poverty, refugees, and prisoners.

• AIDS FOR THE EXERCISES

Dacyczyn, Amy. *Tightwad Gazette*. New York: Villard, 1993.

De Gruchy, John W., ed. *Cry Justice!: Prayers, Meditations and Readings from South Africa*. Maryknoll, N.Y.: Orbis, 1986.

Elgin, Duane. *Voluntary Simplicity: Toward a Way of Life That Is Outwardly Simple, Inwardly Rich*. New York: Wm. Morrow, 1981.

Friesen, Delores Histand. *Living More with Less: Study/Action Guide*. Scottdale, Pa.: Herald, 1981.

Longacre, Doris Janzen. *Living More with Less*. Scottdale, Pa.: Herald, 1980.

Schramm, Mary. "A Wonderful Word: Enough," *Extravagant Love*. Minneapolis: Augsburg, 1988. Pp. 74-85.

• SUGGESTED READING

Allchin, A. M. *The Kingdom of Love and Knowledge: The Encounter between Orthodoxy and the West*. New York: Seabury, 1982.

Brown, Robert McAfee. *Spirituality and Liberation: Overcoming the Great Fallacy*. Louisville: Westminster, 1988.

Cummings, Charles. *Eco-Spirituality: Toward a Reverent Life*. New York: Paulist, 1991.

Donovan, Vincent J. *Christianity Rediscovered: An Epistle from the Masai*. Notre Dame, Ind.: Fides/Claretian, 1978.

Dyrness, William A. *Learning about Theology from the Third World*. Grand Rapids: Zondervan, 1990.

Ferguson, Duncan, ed. *New Age Spirituality: An Assessment*. Louisville, Ky.: Westminster/John Knox, 1993.

Gutierrez, Gustavo. *We Drink from Our Own Wells: The Spiritual Journey of a People*. Maryknoll, N.Y.: Orbis, 1984.

Ilunga, Bakole Wa. *Paths of Liberation: A Third World Spirituality*. Maryknoll, N.Y.: Orbis, 1984.

Koyama, Kosuke. *Waterbuffalo Theology*. London: SCM, 1974.

————. *Three Mile an Hour God*. London: SCM, 1979.

May, Gerald G. *Addiction and Grace*. San Francisco: Harper, 1988.

Neal, Marie Augusta, S.N.D. deN. *A Socio-Theology of Letting Go: The Role of a First World Church Facing Third World Peoples*. New York: Paulist, 1977.

Rakoczy, Susan, ed. *Common Journey, Different Paths: Spiritual Direction in Cross-Cultural Perspective.* Maryknoll, N.Y.: Orbis, 1992.
Shorter, Aylward. *African Christian Spirituality.* New York: Macmillan, 1978.
Timmerman, Joan H. *Sexuality and Spiritual Growth.* New York: Crossroad, 1992.
Underhill, Evelyn. *Mysticism: A Study in the Nature and Development of Man's Spiritual Consciousness.* New York: Dutton, 1961 (first published 1911).

8 | *Where Do We Go from Here?*

There are many ways of analyzing the story I have just told. It is an incomplete story, unwieldy, with rough edges. Each of us will draw our own conclusions. The basic premise of this overview is that we who live today are in continuity with the past and with others throughout the world. There are no "good old days" in the sense of sentimental longing for a perfect time. Rather, the story goes on with ever new challenges and hopes. We have the privilege of knowing the story better than any previous generation. How we understand it, however, is not automatic and easy.

Looking Back Over the Story

Christian spirituality is a style of walking in the Holy Spirit. It therefore involves the whole of life, not some private segment. It is our relationship with God, ourselves, others, and the creation. The Bible gives a potpourri of normative principles, positive and negative examples of life experience, and the gospel of Jesus Christ on which all else depends.

The early centuries of Christianity were characterized by an expansion to many cultures, Asian, African, and European. Within the Roman Empire and in other places, severe persecutions marked Christianity from the beginning. The Jewish affirmation of creation was frequently dimmed and sometimes lost, leaving a legacy of denigration of the body, sexuality, and women in the tradition. The spiritual and moral disciplines of the faith were emphasized by many writers, as well as the growth of mystical communion or union with God.

The Eastern part of the Roman Empire, later called Byzantine, developed in different ways from the West, emphasizing the Resurrection as victory over death and the *theosis* (or divinization) of humans, rather than focusing on the cross as redemption from sin and the forgiveness of guilt as in the West. The icon and the Jesus Prayer, in the context of the divine liturgy with its Eucharist, came to characterize Eastern spirituality, which has constantly renewed itself by going back to the Holy Tradition.

Monasticism in the West was a lay protest movement that engendered much Roman Catholic spiritual writing. The ideals of the orders expanded into

service for the world with the mendicant orders of the thirteenth century and
the Jesuits in the sixteenth. The "love of learning and the desire for God"
were developed in the monasteries.

Protestants emerged to challenge the whole Catholic structure, including
its assumptions about spirituality. Their main point was "grace alone, faith
alone, Scripture alone." Protestants started afresh, with various degrees of
borrowing from Catholic spirituality, but always rooted in their understanding
of biblical teaching.

The modern age was a time for throwing off the "superstitions" of both
Catholics and Protestants, or at least fitting them into a new understanding
of the role of reason. On the Protestant side, the traditions developed Puri-
tanism, Pietism, and Evangelicalism as well as the maverick Kierkegaard.
The Catholics centered on personal spirituality, especially the French school,
preceded by the teachings of the maverick Pascal. During this time Christianity
began to spread to continents other than Europe, but the non-European contributions to the church universal were not usually appreciated.

The twentieth century has seen the development of Christian faith on a
global scale, in some sense fulfilling the promise of the first centuries. It is
time now for Christians in Europe and North America to listen not only to
the writers of the past, but also to peoples of the present from different cultural
traditions. This includes peoples of other continents as well as Native Americans and African-Americans. The role of women in the historical development
of Christianity and in the present has been seriously neglected; the male-
dominated tradition has a great deal to learn from women. We can hope for
a future of mutual understanding and cooperation, though that will not happen
without painful struggles toward reconciliation.

Distinguishing the Root Metaphors
of Spirituality

A number of ways have been used to classify types of spirituality. One of
these is to place them on a graph, in which kataphatic and apophatic are at
the left and right, and the heart and mind are at the top and bottom.[1] Such a
chart can be helpful in identifying psychological tendencies in persons or
schools of thought. Another helpful method for people with theological training
is that of Geoffrey Wainwright, who applies H. Richard Niebuhr's well-known
typology from *Christ and Culture* to spirituality.[2]

Here I will not attempt to classify all types of Christian spirituality, but to
illumine certain metaphors that dominate some of the writers and schools of
spirituality discussed above.

In an attempt to understand our lives, we use fundamental images, or root
metaphors. Each image has value but none is adequate by itself. For example,
the Bible pictures God as Rock, Light, and Fortress; Lion, Bear, and Eagle;
King, Father, and Shepherd; Mother, Lover, and Friend. None of these is

adequate for the nature of God, as Pseudo-Dionysius would remind us. The same is true of our pictures of the Christian life.

The basis of Christian life may be pictured as **rescue, redemption, or justification.** "Jesus saves" means most simply that Jesus rescues the sinner from the powers greater than any person: sin and death. Redemption means setting free a slave by purchase. Justification takes place in the courtroom: the guilty one is declared innocent on the basis of another's interceding. All of these metaphors have in common the initiative of God, who loves and frees us from internal and external powers that bind us. Some might argue that these images refer only to the inception of the Christian life, but on the contrary, the most experienced and mature saints have clung to them. Whatever role our efforts play in Christian living, these metaphors imply that the fundamental fact is that we remain in need all our lives and rely on God's love to save, redeem, liberate, and justify. The spiritualities of the Lutheran and Reformed traditions place these metaphors in the center.

Another set of images suggests the process of Christian living. **Growth, unification, and healing** all describe gradual changes. Biological growth in plants and animals is taken as a model of maturing in the Christian walk. A second view is that we are divided as selves, and the Christian life is a matter of being put back together again, both in terms of integrating our person, and in the sense of uniting with God. Third, healing can be both metaphor and reality in Christian spirituality. As metaphor, it suggests that the Christian walk is the process of healing what is diseased or wounded in the same sense that the man on the road to Jericho was cared for by the Samaritan and the innkeeper (Luke 10:25-37). As reality, healing is an important experience for many whose prayers for physical or emotional healing bring noticeable results. Mystics, including Augustine, and Pentacostalists use these images; Augustine uses them as metaphor, Pentacostalists as experience.

Traveling and returning are all involved in the metaphors of **walking, journeying, climbing, and homing.** Living life through time has often been compared to moving through space, as in walking down a road. This is the image used by early Christians who spoke of their religion as "the Way." The journey underlies John Bunyan's classic allegory, *Pilgrim's Progress.* It suggests that we are on the move and have not yet arrived, but that we do have a destination. The image of climbing, whether a mountain or a ladder, is an ancient one, starting in Genesis. It suggests progressing toward God and being able to look back over one's path. This image does have problems, however, for those of us who see grace as the fundamental reality of the walk, from start to finish. It seems to imply an accomplishment that could be a temptation to pride in one's worthiness. Homing as an image does not focus on the travel, but on return and on settling into one's appropriate place. Some feminist writers have preferred this image, while the Roman Catholic medieval tradition has used a Neo-Platonic version of the journey: We came from God, and we are on our return journey to God.

Death and resurrection become metaphors for Christian falling away and repentance, sin and forgiveness, despair and hope. The death and resurrection of Jesus are seen as the type, or the powerful first instance of this pattern. Luther often spoke of daily baptism in these terms (see Rom. 6:1-11). One might also consider the cycle of Israel's departure from God and return as fitting here.

We are told that a monk given thirty seconds to describe life in his monastery for a television interviewer replied, "We fall down, then we get up. We fall down, then we get up. We fall down, then we get up. We fall down, then we get up. . . ."

Battle has been a recurring image in discussions of Christian spirituality. The writer of Ephesians advises Christians to put on the whole armor of God to be able to stand against the wiles of the devil. Another view of the battle is Paul's internal struggle; different parts of himself are struggling in Romans 7. Later writers expanded on the theme of fighting with spiritual powers, with the "old self," and with the powers of the world. Antony entered the desert to do battle with Satan in the power of Christ. Starting with Johann Arndt, Pietist and Evangelical writers have been accustomed to this image.

Finally, **thirst and hunger** suggest human need for the divine. Human beings are not self-sufficient, however much they may seek to be. Only God is able to supply the "bread of life" (John 6) and "water of life" (John 7). The celebration may even demand wine at times (John 3)!

These metaphors all help to give shape to our experiences; they give us a handle on interpreting our lives. Each needs the others; none is adequate by itself.

Questions About the Global
Christian Community

One basic premise of this discussion is that Christianity is by nature a global rather than a European faith. We have looked at a few developments in selected continents to show that Christians can learn from one another across cultural, linguistic, and racial lines.

But we must also say that even this glimpse of the variety of spiritualities leaves us with certain pressing questions. Among the first is the question of **unity in diversity.** Given that there are different styles of Christian living, can one speak of Christianity as a single religion? Isn't there a serious tension between the social activism of liberation theology and the quiet mysticism of Asian Christian mystics who use the methods of Hinduism or Buddhism?

A related question is how to evaluate different schools of spirituality from different cultures. Our basic stance in this book has been appreciation, welcoming the riches of different cultures to the global Christian family. But each of us must make choices about the life-styles he or she adopts. This also applies cross-culturally. **What are the criteria** for deciding if a given spirituality is authentically Christian and if it is worthy to be emulated outside its own home? If North Americans have much to learn from Latin America, do Asians and Africans also have much to learn from each other?

Are the criteria for evaluating a spirituality the same or different from those for evaluating a theology? I would expect an authentic theology to reflect the Scriptures; to give a central role for Jesus as the Christ; to value faith, hope, and love; to be understandable within its culture; and to challenge the idols of that culture. Are there additional criteria for spiritualities?

A third question concerns the method of transmitting spiritualities cross-culturally. Writing books can be helpful, but books seldom communicate beyond the specialist reader. Music, art, and stories are effective ways of appreciating the spirit of another people, but the exchange of living persons across cultural boundaries is perhaps the best means of sharing spiritualities. Visitors from another continent can best represent living options. How can we more effectively share with one another what the Spirit has given us?

Finally, one of the fundamental issues for our future discussions will be if and how the Christian church can learn from **non-Christian movements and religions** to enhance its own spirituality. Has God given wisdom to other religious traditions? If so, how can Christians value and learn from them without diluting the integrity of their own tradition? I believe that we take for granted much that has been learned from other traditions in the past. Yet there have also been cases in which adopting a spirituality from the outside has led to a distortion of the gospel, for example, Neo-Platonism in European Christianity.

What Is Needed in Our Day?

Just as each period and culture in the history of Christian spirituality is unique, so we as individuals are different from one another. In our thirst for God, we need not all drink from the same kind of cup, glass, or goblet. A survey like this is intended to display the varieties of containers but also to raise questions about their appropriateness for a given setting. Not all of them will be appropriate for North America on the verge of the twenty-first century.

A Christian spirituality for our time must keep the **four relationships** in balance. Much of the Christian tradition has focused on God and others, distorting the relationships to self and creation. Neglecting creation can result in a disparagement of the self as well. Separating the creation relationship from the others, however, can lead to fanatical views, for example, bombing for the sake of animal rights. Each of the four needs the others.

We also need a **listening spirituality.** We must be willing to hear the voices from continents and ages other than our own. It will be important that we

also listen judiciously to peoples of other faiths. In North America this especially means listening to the native peoples of the continent, to women,
and to people recovering from addictions. Without abandoning Christian commitments, it is possible to learn about spirituality that is ecologically healthy
and wholistically physical.

The focus of Christian spirituality must be **Trinitarian.** A strong emphasis
on the Creator needs to supplement our clear, central devotion to Jesus Christ
as incarnate Redeemer, Servant, Healer, and Friend. The role of the Holy
Spirit needs strong emphasis not only for the use of spiritual gifts of many
kinds but also for the sense of the Presence of a powerful and loving God.

The basis of our spirituality in **God's passionate love** must be preserved
against the constant tendency to make spirituality into a meritorious work.
There is no doubt that we are called upon to respond to God's love. From
the perspective of the onlooker, the behavior of the Christian is what counts;
spirituality is a behavior insofar as it involves praying, sharing one's goods,
meditating, advocating the rights of the oppressed, going on retreats, receiving
the sacraments, living simply, witnessing for the faith, reading the Bible, and
so on. Yet all of this is grounded not in our worthy intentions, but in God's
forgiveness, God's empowerment, and God's creation.

The Christian tradition has had serious blind spots. It is not that we in our
day have none, but distance gives us a better perspective on those of other
ages and cultures. One of those has been the acceptance of social norms about
women that Jesus would not have approved. Others are the exploitation of
creation and the neglect of justice for the poor. Finally is the negation of a
proper self-love that nourishes and has patience and forgiveness for oneself.
Each of these blind spots was overcome in some part of the tradition, yet on
the whole, the tradition still needs more correcting.

A Personal Word

As I sit before my computer surrounded by books on a snowy Minnesota day,
I am very much aware that this account of the tradition is only an introduction.

I have tried to give a balanced account of the Orthodox, Catholic, and
Protestant traditions. Including elements from all of them is important, I think,
just as it is important to be aware of the whole Bible. Some parts that may
not seem very useful at one time may be just what is needed at another. For
example, note how Lamentations and the lament Psalms fit with what contemporary psychologists have learned about our need to grieve. I also think
of the increasing role of Orthodox icons and the Jesus Prayer for Western
Christians. And I think of the spiritual power of African and Latin American
Christianity for renewing North American Christians.

Each of us across time and space needs the others.

We have looked now at the story of Christian spirituality in many ages
and lands. It has been an introduction to a world of study and prayer that

invites us to drink deeper. Our thirst for God reflects a chronic dehydration, but God is longing to give us drink.

What then shall we do? Having a wider horizon for our practice of the Christian life, it is up to each of us to select, to experiment, to evaluate, to adapt. A kind of knowledge is available to us from books, but personal knowledge, the kind that really counts, can come only from experience. As my spiritual director likes to say, "Spirituality is not just something to study, but something to live!"

• DISCUSSION QUESTIONS

1. Which parts of this story of Christian spirituality do you find most engaging, and which parts do you find most troublesome?

2. Which of the root metaphors are important to your own spirituality? Why?

3. What are the barriers to cross-cultural exchange among Christians? How can they be overcome?

4. What stance should Christians take toward spiritualities of other religions and of nonreligious movements?

5. Compare your own hopes for spiritualities of the future with those of the author.

• EXERCISES: Service and Vocation

1. On the basis of your love for other people, volunteer your time to help those in need. There is a vast array of opportunities for North Americans. For example, one may help a shelter for battered women; help staff a center that gives food, clothing, or shelter to the homeless; or tutor students with their school lessons or in learning English. Interaction with other people is an important spiritual exercise that feeds into the life of prayer.

2. You are called by God to trust God's love, to act with love for others. You have a calling as a parent or child. You may also be called to a particular occupation in order to reflect these prior calls. Working in the world, whether in the home, office, school, or factory is a vocation from God. Spirituality involves the way one views one's work to express the core of one's values. Consider how your work experience with all of its difficulties can be the place where creative accomplishment and compassion give glory to God.

• AIDS FOR THE EXERCISES

Diehl, William E. *The Monday Connection: A Spirituality of Competence, Affirmation, and Support in the Workplace.* San Francisco: Harper, 1991.

Heiges, Donald. *The Christian's Calling.* 2d ed. Philadelphia: Fortress, 1984.

Hordy, Lee. *The Fabric of This World.* Grand Rapids, Mich.: Eerdmans, 1990.

• SUGGESTED READING

Companions for the Journey Series from St. Mary's Press. Winona, Minn. *Praying with . . . Hildegard of Bingen, Catherine of Sienna, Julian of Norwich,* etc.

Ofstedal, Paul, ed. *Daily Readings from Spiritual Classics.* Minneapolis: Augsburg, 1990.

Appendix: TIME LINE

A.D. 100	(about 50-130)	New Testament
	(about 100)	*Odes of Solomon*
	(about 157)	Montanus
	(160? 220?)	**Ignatius of Antioch**
	(160?-225)	**Tertullian**
	(185-254)	Origen
A.D. 200	(250-353)	Antony
	(296?-373)	Athanasius
A.D. 300	(306?-373)	Ephrem
	(330-379)	Basil of Caesarea
	(345?-399)	Evagrius of Pontus
	(354 430)	Augustine
	(360?-432)	John Cassian
A.D. 400	(480?-547)	Benedict
A.D. 500-1000	(1090-1153)	Bernard of Clairvaux
	(1033-1109)	Anselm of Canterbury
A.D. 1100	(1109-1179)	Hildegard of Bingen
	(1170?-1221)	Dominic Guzman
	(1181/2-1226)	Francis of Assisi
	(1193-1253)	Clare of Assisi
A.D. 1200	(1225-1274)	Thomas Aquinas
	(1260?-1328?)	Meister Eckhart
	(1293-1381)	Jan van Ruysbroeck
	(1296-1359)	Gregory Palamas
A.D. 1300	(1353-1416?)	Julian of Norwich
	(1380-1471)	Thomas à Kempis
A.D. 1400	(1483-1546)	Martin Luther
	(1484-1531)	Ulrich Zwingli
	(1491?-1556)	Ignatius of Loyola
	(1496?-1561)	Menno Simons

A.D. 1500	(1509-1564)	John Calvin
	(1515-1582)	Teresa of Avila
	(1542-1591)	John of the Cross
	(1555-1621)	Johann Arndt
	(1567-1622)	Francis de Sales
	(1575-1629)	Pierre de Berulle
	(1593-1633)	George Herbert
A.D. 1600	(1611-1691)	Lawrence of the Resurrection
	(1623-1662)	Blaise Pascal
	(1624-1691)	George Fox
	(1628-1688)	John Bunyan
	(1635-1705)	Philip Jacob Spener
	(1648-1717)	Mme. Guyon
	(1651-1715)	François Fenelon
	(1663-1727)	August Herman Francke
A.D. 1700	(1703-1791)	John Wesley
	(1707-1788)	Charles Wesley
	(1720-1772)	John Woolman
	(1725-1807)	John Newton
	(1731-1805)	Macarius of Corinth
	(1749-1809)	Nicodemus of the Holy Mountain
	(1759-1833)	William Wilberforce
	(1799-1873)	Henry Venn
A.D. 1800	(1813-1855)	Søren Kierkegaard
	(1866-1929)	William Wade Harris
	(1870-1922)	William Seymour
	(1875-1941)	Evelyn Underhill
A.D. 1900	(1906-1945)	Dietrich Bonhoeffer
	(1910-)	Mother Teresa
	(1915-1968)	Thomas Merton
	(1928-)	Gustavo Gutierrez
	(1929-1968)	Martin Luther King, Jr.
	(1929-)	Kosuke Koyama
	(1931-)	Desmond Tutu
A.D. 2000		

GLOSSARY

anamchara. A Celtic word for "soul friend," a spiritual companion and guide.

anchorite, anchoress. A man or woman who chooses to live alone to pray and meditate.

Anglican. Relating to the Church of England.

apatheia. Literally "passionlessness." In practice, freedom from those passions that drive one away from God.

apophatic. An approach to spirituality that emphasizes the mystery of God and therefore strips away all words and metaphors for God in order to meet God in silence and darkness. See kataphatic.

cenobitic. Communal monasticism as opposed to individual; opposite of eremitic.

Chalcedon. A church council in 451 that defined Jesus Christ as one Person with two natures, human and divine.

charism, charismatic. A charism is a gracious gift from God, such as those discussed by Paul in 1 Corinthians 12. Charismatic Christians value and employ these gifts. Charismatic may more specifically refer to those people in historic denominations who employ these gifts, in distinction from Pentecostalists, who have founded denominations that employ them. In a wider sense, every Christian is charismatic, having received such gifts.

contextualize. To develop a form of Christianity that is culturally fitting.

docetic. Refers to the idea that Jesus only appeared to be human; affirms that spirit must not come into contact with body; one aspect of Gnosticism.

Eastern Orthodox. Those churches such as Greek Orthodox or Russian Orthodox that accept the first seven ecumenical councils as valid, including the definition of Chalcedon. (Roman Catholics accept more councils than seven.)

ecumenical. *1.* Referring to the whole inhabited world, universal. *2.* The movement to unite different Christian denominations.

eremitic. The form of monasticism in which persons live alone. The word *hermit* comes from this word.

Gnosticism. A variety of religious movements judged to be heretical by the early church. They denied the goodness of the world and taught a secret knowledge for escaping from creation at death.

Hellenism. A general word for the Greek culture spread widely by Alexander the Great in the fourth century B.C.

icon. A painting of a religious figure that serves as a point of contact with the worshiper; an object of devotion, but not worship, that affirms the incarnation of Christ.

incarnation. The teaching that the Word became flesh in Jesus of Nazareth; a strong affirmation of the goodness of human, physical life. Not to be confused with *re*incarnation in Hinduism.

Jansenism. A religious movement in seventeenth-century France that taught the predestination of the saved and the unsaved.

justification. Being made right with God; or the declaration that one is righteous on the basis of Christ's death and resurrection; a gift to be received by faith.

kataphatic. An approach to spirituality that makes full use of words and images to describe God. See apophatic.

liberation theology. A movement that sees the goal of the gospel as human freedom from spiritual, political, and economic oppression. May be applied by any oppressed group, e.g., Women's Liberation, Black Liberation, etc.

martyr. A witness to the faith who is put to death.

mendicant. Begging; a characteristic of early Franciscan and Dominican Orders in their desire to embrace a life of voluntary poverty.

monasticism. A movement to seek Christian perfection by leaving one's society and devoting oneself to worship, prayer, and good works. May be practiced alone or in community.

Montanism. Following Montanus, a movement that had very strict ascetical standards, the expectation of the imminent return of Christ, and the practice of charismatic phenomena, especially prophecy.

mysticism. A type of spirituality that seeks union with God or the Ultimate. As commonly used, it may include any supernatural phenomena such as visions and voices, but Christian mystics warned against centering attention on these.

Neo-Platonism. A later form of Plato's teaching developed by Plotinus and others, with a more mystical and religious emphasis than Plato's original philosophy.

Nicea. The Council of Nicea in 325 was the first Ecumenical Council, called by Emperor Constantine to settle doctrinal disputes between divided Christians. Among other things, the council agreed to a statement that the Son was of the same Being as the Father. This later became the basis for the statement we know as the Nicene Creed, a fundamental development in the doctrine of the Trinity.

GLOSSARY

Oriental Orthodox. Churches in Asia and Africa that did not accept the definitions of Chalcedon and came to be separated from the Eastern Orthodox churches, for example, the Ethiopian Church.

pantheism. The view that all things are God and God is all things. The distinction between Creator and creation is eliminated.

panentheism. The view that God is in all things and all things are in God.

paradox. A striking truth that is expressed in seemingly contradictory statements.

Pelagianism. Following Pelagius, a view that people are capable and responsible for working out their own salvation instead of needing to rely solely on God's grace for salvation. This view was opposed by Augustine and later by the Protestant churches.

Philokalia. "The love of beauty"; title of collections of Eastern spiritual writings first by Basil in the fourth century and later by others in the eighteenth century.

Pietism. A renewal movement in seventeenth century Lutheran and Reformed churches that emphasized Bible study, conversion, home prayer meetings, institutions to help the needy, friendship across denominational lines, and world mission. The movement later was seen as legalistic, separatist, and sentimental; the word is commonly used to refer to this latter type of spirituality.

Quietism. A movement in seventeenth-century Roman Catholicism that was condemned for its alleged indifference to all things, including personal salvation.

rosary. A set of beads with a small crucifix used as a devotional aid by Roman Catholics and others to pray the Hail Mary and Our Father prayers while meditating on the events of Mary's and Jesus' lives.

Trent. A council of the Roman Catholic Church that responded to the Protestant Reformation. It was held in Trent, northern Italy, from 1548 to 1563.

Vatican II. The Second Vatican Council, held in Rome at the Vatican from 1962 to 1965.

Western church. The church of the western Mediterranean, specifically the Roman Catholic Church, and later the Protestant churches that separated from it.

NOTES

1: SPIRITUALITY AND CHRISTIANITY

1. John, chapter 4.
2. John 7:37-39.
3. Henry Nouwen, "Foreword" to Gustavo Gutierrez, *We Drink from Our Own Wells* (Maryknoll, N.Y.: Orbis, 1984), xx, xxi.
4. Gordon S. Wakefield, ed. *Westminster Dictionary of Christian Spirituality* (Philadelphia: Westminster, 1983), v.
5. Ibid., 361-62.
6. Jaroslav Pelikan, *The Vindication of Tradition* (New Haven: Yale University Press, 1984), 65.
7. C. S. Lewis, "Introduction" in *The Incarnation of the Word of God: Being the Treatise of St. Athanasius De Incarnatione Verbi Dei* (New York: Macmillan, 1947), 6-7.

3: THE BEGINNINGS OF A GLOBAL COMMUNITY

1. James Hamilton Charlesworth, ed., *The Old Testament Pseudepigrapha*, vol. 2 (Garden City, N.Y.: Doubleday, 1985), 726-27.
2. Ibid., 749.
3. Ibid., 752-53.
4. Tertullian, *Disciplinary, Moral and Ascetical Works* (New York: Fathers of the Church, Inc., 1959), 103.
5. Sebastian Brock, "Introduction" in Saint Ephrem's *Hymns on Paradise* (Crestwood, N.Y.: St. Vladimir's Seminary Press, 1990), 25-32.
6. Ibid., 40.
7. Ibid., 48.
8. Ibid., 73. Quotation from Hymns on Virginity (48.17-18).
9. See, e.g., Benedicta Ward's translation, *The Desert Christian: Sayings of the Desert Fathers: The Alphabetical Collection* (New York: Macmillan, 1980), or Thomas Merton's selection, *The Wisdom of the Desert: Sayings from the Desert Fathers of the Fourth Century* (Norfolk, Conn.: New Directions, 1960). Also see Helen Waddell's *The Desert Fathers* (New York: Sheed and Ward, 1942).
10. Ward, trans., *The Desert Christian*, 72.
11. Ibid., 193.
12. Ibid., 194.

138   NOTES

13. Ibid., 196.
14. Gregory of Nyssa, "Life of St. Macrina," in *Ascetical Works, Fathers of the Church*, vol. 58 (Washington, D.C.: Catholic University of America Press, 1966), 163-91.
15. Kallistos Ware, "Ways of Prayer and Contemplation: I. Eastern" in McGinn and Meyendorff, eds. *Christian Spirituality: Origins to the Twelfth Century* (New York: Crossroad, 1987), 398.
16. Ludwig Bieler, trans., *The Works of St. Patrick* (Ancient Christian Writers Series, Westminster, Md.: Newman Press, 17, 1953), 70-71.
17. Edward C. Sellner, *Mentoring: The Ministry of Spiritual Kinship* (Notre Dame, Ind.: Ave Maria, 1990), 61-75.
18. Pseudo-Dionysius, "The Divine Names," chap. 1, in *Pseudo-Dionysius: The Complete Works* (New York: Paulist, 1987), 49-50.
19. "The Mystical Theology," chap. 1, in *Pseudo-Dionysius: The Complete Works*, 135.

4: THE EUROPEAN ERA

1. Kallistos Ware, "The Origins of the Jesus Prayer: Diadochus, Gaza, Sinai," in *The Study of Spirituality*, ed. Cheslyn Jones, Geoffrey Wainwright, and Edward Yarnold (New York: Oxford University Press, 1986), 176.
2. Ibid., 184.
3. Henry R. Percival, ed. *The Seven Ecumenical Councils of the Undivided Church*. A Select Library of Nicene and Post-Nicene Fathers of the Christian Church, Second Series, vol. 14 (Grand Rapids, Mich.: Eerdmans, 1959), 550.
4. Athanasius, "On the Incarnation of the Word," *The Christology of the Later Fathers*, ed. E. R. Hardy (Philadelphia: Westminster, 1954), 55-110.
5. *Anselm, Proslogion*, chap. 2.
6. Thomas Merton. *The Last of the Fathers: Saint Bernard of Clairvaux and the Encyclical Letter, Doctor Mellifluus* (New York: Harcourt, Brace, 1954), 93.
7. Bernard of Clairvaux, *On Loving God*, chaps. 8-11.
8. Bernard of Clairvaux, *Sermons on the Song of Songs*, Sermon 69 (London: SCM, 1959), 117-18.
9. Ingrid H. Shafer, *Eros and the Womanliness of God: Andrew Greeley's Romances of Renewal* (Chicago: Loyola University Press, 1986).
10. Bernard, *Song of Songs*, 108-9.
11. Thomas à Kempis, *The Imitation of Christ* (Baltimore: Penguin Books, 1975) 3:37.
12. Matthew Fox, O.P., *Breakthrough: Meister Eckhart's Creation Spirituality in New Translation* (Garden City, N.Y.: Image Books, 1980), 39.
13. John Ruusbroec, *The Spiritual Espousals and Other Works* (New York: Paulist, 1985), 70.
14. Ibid., 167.
15. Ibid., 182.
16. Ibid., 77.
17. Julian of Norwich, *Showings*, Long Text, chaps. 52-63.
18. Julian of Norwich, *Showings* (New York: Paulist, 1978), 342.

5: PROTESTANT AND CATHOLIC REFORM

1. Bengt R. Hoffman, *Luther and the Mystics: A Re-examination of Luther's Spiritual Experience and His Relation to the Mystics* (Minneapolis: Augsburg, 1976).

2. Martin Luther, *The Freedom of a Christian*, in *Martin Luther' Basic Theological Writings*, ed. Timothy F. Lull (Minneapolis: Fortress, 1989), 596.

3. Walter Trobisch, "Martin Luther's Quiet Time," *Complete Works of Walter Trobisch* (Downers Grove, Ill.: InterVarsity Press, 1987), 703-714.

4. "Sermon on Job," vol. 34, col. 316; "Commentary on Isaiah 42:14," vol. 36, col. 69. John Calvin, *Opera Quae Supersunt Omnia* (Braunschweig: C. A. Schwetschke, 1863-1900. Corpus Reformatorum Series, reprint New York: Johnson Reprint Corporation, 1964).

5. Paul V. Marshall, in *Protestant Spiritual Traditions*, ed. Frank C. Senn (New York: Paulist, 1986), 133.

6. *The Collected Works of St. John of the Cross*, trans. Kieran Kavanaugh and Otilio Rodriguez (Washington, D.C.: Institute of Carmelite Studies Publications, 1979), 711-12.

6: THE "MODERN ERA"

1. John Wesley, *The Journals of John Wesley: A Selection*, ed. Elisabeth Jay (New York: Oxford University Press, 1987), 34-35.

2. Charles Wesley, *Lutheran Book of Worship*, (Minneapolis: Augsburg Publishing House, 1978), 559.

3. Brother Lawrence of the Resurrection, *The Practice of the Presence of God* (Westminster, Md.: Newman Press, 1952), 107.

4. Thomas Merton, "Reflections on the Character and Genius of Fenelon," in *Fenelon's Letters of Love and Counsel* (New York: Harcourt, Brace, and World, 1964), 9-30.

5. Ibid., 216-18.

6. Ibid., 289.

7. *The Way of a Pilgrim: and the Pilgrim Continues His Way*, trans. R. M. French (New York: Harper, 1952), 6-9.

7: THE TWENTIETH CENTURY

1. David B. Barrett, ed. *World Christian Encyclopedia: A Comparative Study of Churches and Religions in the Modern World A.D. 1900-2000.* (New York: Oxford University Press, 1982), 1-20.

2. William A. Dyrness, *Learning about Theology from the Third World* (Grand Rapids: Zondervan, 1990).

3. Susan Rakoczy, IHM, *Common Journey, Different Paths: Spiritual Direction in Cross-Cultural Perspective* (Maryknoll, N.Y.: Orbis, 1992).

4. Vincent J. Donovan, *Christianity Rediscovered: An Epistle from the Masai* (Notre Dame, Ind.: Fides/Claretian, 1978).

5. Jon Sobrino, *Spirituality of Liberation: Toward Political Holiness* (Maryknoll, N.Y.: Orbis, 1988).

6. Bukole Wa Ilunga, *Paths of Liberation: A Third World Spirituality* (Maryknoll, N.Y.: Orbis, 1985), 36.

7. Charles Villa-Vicentio, *Trapped in Apartheid* (Grand Rapids: Eerdmans, 1989).

8. John W. De Gruchy, ed., *Cry Justice! Prayers, Meditations and Readings from South Africa* (Maryknoll, N.Y.: Orbis, 1986).

9. Ibid., 64-66.

10. Zephania Kameeta, *Why, O Lord? Psalms and Sermons from Namibia* (Philadelphia: Fortress, 1986), 30.

11. Gordon Mackay Haliburton, *The Prophet Harris: A Study of an African Prophet and His Mass-Movement in the Ivory Coast and the Gold Coast 1913-1915* (New York: Oxford University Press, 1973).

12. Kosuke Koyama, *Waterbuffalo Theology* (Maryknoll, N.Y.: Orbis Books, 1974).

13. Kosuke Koyama, *Three Mile an Hour God* (Maryknoll, N.Y.: Orbis Books, 1980).

14. Kosuke Koyama, *Mount Fuji and Mount Sinai: A Critique of Idols* (Maryknoll, N.Y.: Orbis, 1984).

15. Dennis C. Morreim, *Changed Lives: The Story of Alcoholics Anonymous* (Minneapolis: Augsburg, 1992).

16. Ernest Kurtz, *Not-God: A History of Alcoholics Anonymous* (Center City, Minn.: Hazelden, 1979).

17. *Alcoholics Anonymous*, 3d ed. (New York: A.A. World Services), 59-60. The Twelve Steps are reprinted with permission of Alcoholics Anonymous World Services, Inc. Permission to reprint this does not mean that AA has reviewed or approved the contents of this publication, nor that AA agrees with the views expressed herein. AA is a program of recovery from alcoholism—use of the Twelve Steps in connection with programs and activities which are patterned after AA, but which address other problems, does not imply otherwise.

18. Dennis C. Morreim, *The Road to Recovery: Bridges Between the Bible and the Twelve Steps* (Minneapolis: Augsburg, 1990).

19. Reinhold Niebuhr. "Written for a service in the Congregational Church of Heath, Massachusetts, where Dr. Niebuhr spent many summers, the prayer was first published in a monthly bulletin of the Federal Council of Churches." John Bartlett, *Familiar Quotations*, 15th ed. (Boston: Little, Brown, 1980), 823.

20. Gerald May, *Addiction and Grace* (San Francisco: Harper, 1988).

21. Matthew Fox, O.P., *Breakthrough: Meister Eckhart's Creation Spirituality in New Translation* (Garden City, N.Y.: Image Books, 1980), 43-48.

22. Ibid., 4.

23. Matthew Fox, "Creation Centered Spirituality," *Westminster Dictionary of Christian Spirituality* (Philadelphia: Westminster, 1983), 100.

8: WHERE DO WE GO FROM HERE?

1. Allan H. Sager, *Gospel-Centered Spirituality: An Introduction to Our Spiritual Journey* (Minneapolis: Augsburg, 1990), 36.

2. Cheslyn Jones, Geoffrey Wainwright, and Edward Yarnold, eds., *The Study of Spirituality* (New York: Oxford University Press, 1986), 592-605.

Bibliography

Allchin, A. M. *The Kingdom of Love and Knowledge: The Encounter between Orthodoxy and the West.* New York: Seabury, 1982.

Appasamy, A. J. *Christianity as Bhakti Marga: A Study in the Mysticism of the Johannine Writings.* London: Macmillan, 1927.

——————. *The Gospel and India's Heritage.* London: SPCK, 1942.

Bernard of Clairvaux. *On Loving God: and Selections from Sermons.* London: SCM, 1959.

Bieler, Ludwig, trans., *The Works of St. Patrick.* Westminster, Md.: Newman Press, Ancient Christian Writers Series, 17, 1953. Pp. 70-71.

Bosch, David J. *Transforming Mission: Paradigm Shifts in Theology of Mission.* Maryknoll, N.Y.: Orbis, 1991.

Bouyer, Louis, et al. *Orthodox Spirituality and Protestant and Anglican Spirituality. History of Christian Spirituality.* Vol. 3. New York: Desclee, 1969.

——————. *The Spirituality of the New Testament and the Fathers. History of Christian Spirituality.* Vol. 1. New York: Desclee, 1964.

Boyd, R. H. S. *An Introduction to Indian Christian Theology.* Madras: Christian Literature Society, 1969.

Brock, Sebastian, trans. *The Syriac Fathers on Prayer and the Spiritual Life.* Kalamazoo, Mich.: Cistercian, 1987.

Brooks, Peter, ed. *Christian Spirituality: Essays in Honour of Gordon Rupp.* London: SCM Press, 1975.

Bynum, Caroline Walker. *Jesus as Mother: Studies in the Spirituality of the High Middle Ages.* Berkeley, Calif.: University of California Press, 1982.

Charlesworth, James Hamilton, ed. and trans. *The Odes of Solomon: The Syriac Texts.* Society of Biblical Literature, Texts and Translations 13, Pseudepigrapha Series 7. Missoula, Mont.: Scholars Press, 1977. Pp. 70-71.

Christensen, Bernhard. *The Inner Pilgrimage.* Minneapolis: Augsburg, 1975.

Dacyczyn, Amy. *Tightwad Gazette.* New York: Villard, 1993.

de Sales, Francis. *Introduction to the Devout Life.* Garden City, N.Y.: Image Books, 1972.

Donovan, Vincent J. *Christianity Rediscovered: An Epistle from the Masai.* Notre Dame, Ind.: Fides/Claretian, 1978.

Dupre, Louis, and Don E. Saliers, eds. *Christian Spirituality: Post Reformation and Modern. World Spirituality.* Vol. 18. New York: Crossroad, 1989.

142 BIBLIOGRAPHY

Elder, E. Rozanne, ed. *The Spirituality of Western Christendom*. Kalamazoo, Mich.: Cistercian, 1976.

Elgin, Duane, *Voluntary Simplicity: Toward a Way of Life That Is Outwardly Simple, Inwardly Rich*. New York: Wm. Morrow, 1981.

Erb, Peter C., ed. *The Pietists: Selected Writings*. Classics of Western Spirituality Series. New York: Paulist, 1983.

Ferguson, Duncan, ed. *New Age Spirituality: An Assessment*. Louisville, Ky.: Westminster/John Knox, 1993.

Fremantle, Anne, ed. *The Protestant Mystics*. New York: New American Library, 1964.

French, R. M., trans. *The Way of a Pilgrim: and the Pilgrim Continues His Way*. New York: Harper, 1952.

Friesen, Delores Histand, *Living More with Less: Study/Action Guide*. Scottdale, Pa.: Herald, 1981.

Gannon, Thomas M., and George W. Traub. *The Desert and the City: An Interpretation of the History of Christian Spirituality*. New York: Macmillan, 1969.

Gonzolez, Justo L. *A History of Christian Thought*. 3 vols. New York: Abingdon, 1970-75.

Graef, Hilda. *The Light and the Rainbow: A Study in Christian Spirituality from Its Roots in the Old Testament and Its Development through the New Testament and the Fathers to Recent Times*. Westminster, Md.: Newman, 1959.

Gutierrez, Gustavo. *We Drink From Our Own Wells: The Spiritual Journey of a People*. Translated by Matthew J. O'Connell. Maryknoll, N.Y.: Orbis Books, 1984.

Hanson, Bradley. *The Call of Silence: Discovering Christian Meditation*. Minneapolis: Augsburg, 1980.

——————. "Christian Spirituality and Spiritual Theology," *Dialog* 21/3 (Summer 1982), 207-12.

——————, ed. *Modern Christian Spirituality: Methodological and Historical Essays*. American Academy of Religion Studies in Religion. No. 62. Atlanta: Scholars Press, 1990.

Hinson, E. Glenn. "The Theory of Spirituality," *One in Christ* 17/3 (1981), 244-49.

Hoffman, Bengt R. *Luther and the Mystics: A Re-examination of Luther's Spiritual Experiences and His Relation to the Mystics*. Minneapolis: Augsburg, 1976.

Holmes, Urban T. III. *A Brief History of Christian Spirituality*. New York: Seabury. 1981.

——————. *Spirituality for Ministry*. San Francisco: Harper and Row, 1982.

Hosmer, Rachel. "Current Literature on Spirituality (Review Article)," *Anglican Theological Review* 66:4, 423-41.

Hulme, William E. *Let the Spirit In: Practicing Christian Devotional Meditation*. Nashville: Abingdon, 1979.

Ilunga, Bakole, Wa. *Paths of Liberation: A Third World Spirituality*. Maryknoll, N.Y.: Orbis, 1984.

Jantzen, Grace M. *Julian of Norwich: Mystic and Theologian*. New York: Paulist, 1988.

Jodock, Darrell. *The Church's Bible: Its Contemporary Authority*. Minneapolis: Fortress, 1989.

Jones, Cheslyn, Geoffrey Wainwright, and Edward Yarnold, eds. *The Study of Spirituality*. New York: Oxford University Press, 1986.

Julian of Norwich, *Showings*. New York: Paulist, 1982.

Jungmann, Joseph A. *Christian Prayer through the Centuries*. Translated by John Coyne. New York: Paulist, 1978.

Kavanaugh, Kieran, and Otilio Rodriguez, eds. *The Collected Works of St. John of the Cross*. Washington, D.C.: Institute of Carmelite Studies Publications, 1979.

Keller, John. *Let Go, Let God*. Minneapolis: Augsburg, 1985.

à Kempis, Thomas. *The Imitation of Christ*. Baltimore: Penguin Books, 1975.

Klug, Ron, and Lyn Klug. *Faithful Hearts, Faithful Hands*. Rejoice Curriculum for Adults. Minneapolis: Augsburg, 1992.

Knowles, David. *Christian Monasticism*. New York: McGraw-Hill, 1969.

_____. *From Pachomius to Ignatius: A Study in the Constitutional History of the Religious Orders*. London: Oxford University Press, 1966.

Koyama, Kosuke. *Waterbuffalo Theology*. Maryknoll, N.Y.: Orbis Books, 1974.

_____. *Three Mile an Hour God*. Maryknoll, N.Y.: Orbis Books, 1979.

Lawrence, C. H. *Medieval Monasticism*. 2d ed. New York: Longman, 1989.

Leclercq, Jean, Francois Vandenbroucke, and Louis Bouyer. *The Spirituality of the Middle Ages*. History of Christian Spirituality. Vol. 2. London: Burns and Oates, 1968.

Leech, Kenneth. *Soul Friend: The Practice of Christian Spirituality*. San Francisco: Harper & Row, 1980.

_____. *True Prayer: An Introduction to Christian Spirituality*. London: Sheldon, 1980.

Luibheid, Colm, trans. *Pseudo-Dionysius: The Complete Works*. New York: Paulist, 1987.

Lundin, Roger, and Mark A. Noll. *Voices from the Heart: Four Centuries of American Piety*. Grand Rapids: Eerdmans, 1987.

Luther, Martin. "A Simple Way to Pray," *Luther's Works*. Vol. 43. Philadelphia: Fortress, 1968. Pp. 187-212.

McCarty, Doran. "Southern Baptist Spirituality," One in Christ 17/3 (1981), 250-54.

_____. "Spirituality: A Southern Baptist Perspective," *Review and Expositer* 79/2 (Spring 1982), 307-11.

McGinn, Bernard, and John Meyendorff, eds. *Christian Spirituality: Origins to the Twelfth Century*. World Spirituality. Vol. 16. New York: Crossroad, 1985.

MacNutt, Francis. *Healing*. Notre Dame, Ind.: Ave Maria, 1974.

Madame Guyon: An Autobiography. Chicago: Moody, n.d.

Marshall, Michael. *The Restless Heart: The Life and Influence of St. Augustine*. Grand Rapids: Eerdmans, 1987.

Merton, Thomas. *The Last of the Fathers: Saint Bernard of Clairvaux and the Encyclical Letter, Doctor Mellifluus*. New York: Harcourt, Brace, 1954.

_____. *The Wisdom of the Desert: Sayings from the Desert Fathers of the Fourth Century*. Norfolk, Conn.: New Directions, 1960.

Meyendorff, John, *Byzantine Theology: Historical Trends and Doctrinal Themes*. New York: Fordham University Press, 1987.

Mott, Michael. *The Seven Mountains of Thomas Merton*. Boston: Houghton Mifflin, 1984.

Mulhearn, Timothy, ed. *Getting It All Together: The Heritage of Thomas Merton*. Wilmington, Del.: Michael Glazier, 1984.

Neal, Maria Augusta, S.N.D. deN. *A Socio-Theology of Letting Go: The Role of a First World Church Facing Third World Peoples*. New York: Paulist, 1977.

Nouwen, Henri J. M. *Heart Speaks to Heart: Three Prayers to Jesus*. Notre Dame, Ind.: Ave Maria, 1989.

——————. *The Living Reminder. Service and Prayer in Memory of Jesus Christ*. New York: Seabury, 1977.

——————. *Making All Things New: An Invitation to the Spiritual Life*. San Francisco: Harper, 1981.

——————. *Reaching Out: The Three Movements of the Spiritual Life*. Garden City, N.Y.: Doubleday, 1975.

——————. *The Way of the Heart: Desert Spirituality and Contemporary Ministry*. New York: Seabury, 1981.

O'Donnell, Joseph. "Spirituality: A Roman Catholic Perspective," *Review and Expositer*. 79/2 (Spring 1982), 293-305.

O'Donnell, Joseph, and Doran McCarty. "Spirituality: An Epilogue," *Review and Expositer*. 79/2 (Spring 1982), 312-13.

Ofstedal, Paul, ed. *Daily Readings from Spiritual Classics*. Minneapolis: Augsburg, 1990.

Pelikan, Jaroslav. *The Christian Tradition: A History of the Development of Doctrine*. 5 vols. Chicago: University of Chicago, 1971-89.

——————. *Jesus through the Centuries: His Place in the History of Culture*. New Haven: Yale University Press, 1985.

——————. *The Vindication of Tradition*. New Haven: Yale University Press, 1984.

Percival, Henry R. ed. *The Seven Ecumenical Councils of the Undivided Church*. A Select Library of Nicene and Post-Nicene Fathers of the Christian Church, Second Series, vol. 14. Grand Rapids, Mich.: Eerdmans, 1959.

Principe, Walter. "Toward Defining Spirituality," *Studies in Religion*. 12/2 (Spring 1983), 127-41.

Raitt, Jill, ed. *Christian Spirituality: High Middle Ages and Reformation*. World Spirituality. Vol. 17. New York: Crossroad, 1987.

Rakoczy, Susan, ed. *Common Journey, Different Paths: Spiritual Direction in Cross-Cultural Perspective*. Maryknoll, N.Y.: Orbis, 1992.

Roberts, Robert C. "What Is Spirituality?" *Reformed Journal*. 33/8 (August 1983), 14-18.

Sager, Allan H. *Gospel-Centered Spirituality: An Introduction to Our Spiritual Journey*. Minneapolis: Augsburg, 1990.

Schramm, Mary. "A Wonderful Word: Enough," *Extravagant Love*. Minneapolis: Augsburg, 1988. Pp. 74-85.

Sellner, Edward C., *Mentoring: The Ministry of Spiritual Kinship*. Notre Dame, Ind.: Ave Maria, 1990.

Senn, Frank C., ed. *Protestant Spiritual Traditions*. New York: Paulist, 1986.

Shafer, Ingrid H. *Eros and the Womanliness of God: Andrew Greeley's Romances of Renewal*. Chicago: Loyola University Press, 1986.

Shorter, Alyward. *African Christian Spirituality*. New York: Macmillan, 1978.

Sittler, Joseph A. "Spirituality and Discipline," *Word and World* 3 (Spring 1983): 123-28.

Spener, Philip Jacob. *Pia Desideria*. Minneapolis: Fortress, 1989 (1964).

Sponheim, Paul R., ed. *A Primer on Prayer*. Philadelphia: Fortress, 1988.

Steere, Douglas V., ed. *Quaker Spirituality: Selected Writings*. Classics of Western Spirituality Series. New York: Paulist, 1984.

Timmerman, Joan H. *Sexuality and Spiritual Growth*. New York: Crossroad, 1992.

Trobisch, Walter. "Martin Luther's Quiet Time," *Complete Works of Walter Trobisch*. Downers Grove, Ill.: InterVarsity Press, 1987. Pp. 703-14.

Tugwell, Simon, O.P. *Ways of Imperfection*. Springfield, Ill.: Templegate, 1985.

van der Bent, Ans. "The Concern for Spirituality: An Analytical and Bibliographical Survey of the Discussion within the WCC Constituency," *Ecumenical Review* 38/1 (January 1986), 101-14.

Volz, Carl A. *Faith and Practice in the Early Church: Foundations for Contemporary Theology*. Minneapolis: Augsburg, 1983.

Waddell, Helen. *The Desert Fathers*. New York: Sheed and Ward, 1942.

Wainwright, Geoffrey. "Christian Spirituality," *The Encyclopedia of Religion*. New York: Macmillan, 3: 452-60.

——————. *Doxology: The Praise of God in Worship, Doctrine, and Life*. New York: Oxford University Press, 1980.

Wakefield, Gordon S., ed. *The Westminster Dictionary of Christian Spirituality*. Philadelphia: Westminster, 1983.

Ward, Benedicta. *The Desert Christian: Sayings of the Desert Fathers: The Alphabetical Collection*. New York: Macmillan, 1980.

Ware, Timothy, ed. *The Art of Prayer: An Orthodox Anthology*. London: Faber, 1966.

Williams, Rowan. *Christian Spirituality: A Theological History from the New Testament to Luther and St. John of the Cross*. Atlanta: John Knox, 1980.

Index of Names

Index of Subjects